This book belongs to

_____

2019
CHRISTMAS
WITH
Southern Living

2019
CHRISTMAS

WITH

Southern Living

Inspired Ideas for
Holiday Cooking & Decorating

Merry Christmas!

Year after year, *Christmas with Southern Living* is a project we get excited about. It starts with a brainstorming meeting to come up with the edition's chapter themes, which inspire the menus and recipes. With that defined, our Test Kitchen gets to work developing delicious recipes while photo stylist Kay Clarke and I turn our focus to the visual direction for each chapter. Editors of this annual series may come and go, but Kay has created the shots in every edition of this book for over 25 years. She has decorated more mantels, trees, doors, and mailboxes than I can tally. Her passion shows in photo after photo, year after year. I have learned important decorating lessons from her along the way—how to make a bow with bountiful loops, squint my eyes to see where more lights are needed on the tree, and to never ever use her ribbon scissors on paper or her flower snips to open a box. To be honest, I've learned important life lessons from her too.

We spend hours planning the look and feel for each chapter of the Entertaining section. It's not unlike what you probably undertake when planning your own holiday menus, table settings, and Christmas decor. We ponder color palettes: Should we go with white and cream with powder blue accents for "Winter Wonderland" (page 10)? We did. We define decorative direction: rustic or refined? A laid-back New Year's breakfast menu made "Ring in the New" (page 86) ideal for a relaxed, rustic vibe.

Once we've defined the visual style for each chapter, we scout locations for photography. Should we shoot "Sterling Traditions" (page 66) in that historic mansion with the fine antiques, or go with the mid-century colonial packed with modern furnishings? We chose the latter to show that heirloom silver mixed with contemporary pieces makes a stunning statement. Sometimes a home's distinctive upholstery, art, or color scheme are tailor-made for a chapter, such as "Visions of Sugarplums" (page 46), which makes our decision to shoot there a cinch. Of course any story comes to life in a home with neutral elements, thoughtful architecture, and loads of natural light. "Cheers to the Season" (page 28) is proof of that.

Once we have all that nailed down, we head "to Market to Market" to buy lots and lots of props—dishes, flatware, linens, ornaments, holiday accents, small furnishings, wrapping paper, ribbon, and so many special elements that will make each chapter come together. It's a lot of work, but it's been a labor of love that Kay Clarke has undertaken with unparalleled passion over decades. I have had such fun being a part of it for over ten years. I hope you enjoy what you find in these pages as much as we enjoyed creating it for you.

Happiest of holidays to you and yours,

Katherine Cobbs
Executive Editor

Contents

Entertain

1

Winter WONDERLAND

WELCOME THE HOLIDAY SEASON WITH A CASUAL
CHRISTMAS LUNCHEON FOR FRIENDS DECKED OUT IN
WINTRY WHITES, POWDERY BLUES, AND CREAMY HUES
FROM ENTRY TO KITCHEN AND SIDEBOARD TO TABLE.

THE MENU
SERVES 12

White Christmas
Tea Punch

White Bean and
Rosemary Soup

Mini Quiches with
Smoked Gouda

Kale Ribbon Salad

Crab Cakes with
Pimiento Rémoulade

Vanilla Bean Pots
de Crème

Chocolate-Dipped
Tuile Cookies

Fur and Frost

Flocked greenery adds a dose
of wintry magic starting at the door.
Go faux, or use flocking spray to
dust real greenery with "snow." A fur
table runner, forest of ceramic trees,
and vases of blooms complement
the tree in the dining room.

Fire and Ice

A lush garland on the mantel makes gathering by the fire more festive. Woodland accents in white—a towering tree on a faux bois table and a wooden buck on the hearth—lend a fanciful feel to the decor.

Get the Look

Repeat decorative elements for impact and drama. Traditional evergreen accents are always found frosted here. Flowers, icy branches, and a flocked garland are softened by waves of ribbon and sprays of frosty pine. Judicious doses of spruce blue offer a fresh counterpoint to the wintry elements. Whimsical accents like a vintage toy pickup, miniature deer, mini trees, and a galvanized tree for display add interest at every turn.

White Christmas Tea Punch

This pleasing punch with subtle tea notes is quick and easy. Mix the base a day before. Top off with the soda and sparkling cider to serve.

1 Bring 4 ½ cups water to a boil in a medium saucepan over high; add tea bags and sugar. Boil 1 minute; remove from heat. Steep 10 minutes.

2 Meanwhile, pour lemon juice through a wire-mesh strainer, discarding any solids. Discard tea bags. Pour tea into a 1-gallon container; add lemon juice and peach nectar. Cover and chill 8 to 24 hours.

3 Pour chilled tea mixture into a punch bowl or pitcher. Gently stir in club soda and sparkling apple cider just before serving. Garnish with lemon slices and mint sprigs.

VARIATION

Spiked White Christmas Tea Punch
Prepare recipe as directed, substituting **1 (750-milliliter) bottle Prosecco** for 4 cups sparkling apple cider. SERVES **12**

SERVES **12**
HANDS-ON **10 MINUTES**
TOTAL **8 HOURS, 15 MINUTES,**
INCLUDING 8 HOURS CHILLING

---

4 ½ cups water

6 green tea bags

1 cup granulated sugar

1 cup fresh lemon juice (from 8 lemons)

1 (33.8-ounce) bottle peach nectar

4 cups club soda, chilled

4 cups sparkling apple cider, chilled

Lemon slices

Mint sprigs

White Bean and Rosemary Soup

SERVES **12**
HANDS-ON **20 MINUTES**
TOTAL **35 MINUTES**

4 thick-cut bacon slices, cut into
  ½-inch pieces

2 ½ cups chopped yellow onion
  (from 1 large onion)

1 cup finely chopped celery
  (from 3 stalks)

3 large garlic cloves, finely
  chopped (about 1 tablespoon)

1 ½ tablespoons chopped fresh
  rosemary

½ cup dry white wine

8 cups chicken broth

2 (15-ounce) cans cannellini
  beans or navy beans, drained
  and rinsed

1 (6-ounce) package fresh baby
  spinach

2 tablespoons fresh lemon juice
  (from 1 lemon)

Kosher salt and black pepper

Hearty, yet light, this brothy soup gets smoky flavor from the bacon, creaminess from the mashed beans, and rosemary imbues it with cozy winter flavor.

1 Cook bacon in a large Dutch oven over medium-high, stirring occasionally, until crispy, about 10 minutes. Using a slotted spoon, transfer bacon to a plate lined with paper towels, reserving drippings in Dutch oven. Set bacon aside.

2 Add onion, celery, and garlic to hot drippings. Cook over medium-high, stirring often, until onions are tender but not browned, about 5 minutes. Stir in rosemary and wine, scraping any browned bits from bottom of Dutch oven. Cook, stirring occasionally, until wine is reduced by half, about 2 minutes. Stir in broth and half of the beans. Bring to a boil, reduce heat to medium-low, and simmer 15 minutes.

3 In a medium bowl, mash remaining half of beans with a fork. Stir mashed beans into mixture in Dutch oven. Stir in spinach, and cook until just wilted, about 3 minutes.

4 Remove from heat; stir in lemon juice and desired amount of salt and pepper. Garnish with cooked bacon.

Mini Quiches with Smoked Gouda

SERVES **12** HANDS-ON **20 MINUTES** TOTAL **35 MINUTES**

Cook the quiches until they are almost set (the very centers are still jiggly) and then remove and cool completely. They will firm up as they cool. If you'd like to make these ahead of time, just refrigerate and then reheat them in a warm oven.

1 (14.1-ounce) package refrigerated piecrusts
4 large eggs
²/₃ cup heavy cream
2 ounces smoked Gouda cheese, grated (about ¹/₂ cup)
¹/₄ cup diced deli ham (1 ¹/₂ ounces)
1 teaspoon chopped fresh thyme
¹/₂ teaspoon kosher salt
¹/₄ teaspoon black pepper

1 Preheat oven to 350°F. Spray 2 (12-cup) miniature muffin pans with cooking spray.

2 On a lightly floured surface, unroll piecrusts. Roll each crust into a 14-inch circle; cut out 24 (3-inch) rounds from crusts, rerolling dough, if necessary. Place 1 (3-inch) round into each miniature muffin cup, pressing crust into bottom and up sides of cup. Cut off any excess so crust is flush with top of cup. Form 24 (2-inch) balls from aluminum foil; place 1 foil ball in each cup. Bake in preheated oven until crusts begin to brown, about 15 minutes. Let crusts cool in pans on wire racks until cool enough to handle, about 10 minutes.

3 Meanwhile, whisk together eggs, cream, cheese, ham, thyme, salt, and pepper in a large bowl until blended. Remove foil balls from crusts. Spoon egg mixture evenly into crusts (about 1 tablespoon plus 1 teaspoon per crust). Bake at 350°F until just set, 13 to 14 minutes. Let cool in pans 10 minutes. Remove from pans, and serve warm or at room temperature.

VARIATION

Crustless Mini Quiches with Smoked Gouda

To make crustless quiches, omit piecrusts. Prepare recipe as directed in Step 1, omitting cooking spray. Line muffin pans with miniature paper liners. Omit Step 2, and proceed as directed in Step 3.

Kale Ribbon Salad

SERVES **12** HANDS-ON **15 MINUTES** TOTAL **25 MINUTES**

Lacinato kale is also called Tuscan kale or dinosaur kale, so it can be confusing in the store. What's great about kale is that, even dressed, it holds nicely in the fridge!

¹/₄ cup rice wine vinegar
¹/₂ cup golden raisins
2 (6- to 7-ounce) bunches lacinato kale, stemmed
1 ounce Parmigiano-Reggiano cheese, shaved (about ¹/₂ cup)
1 cup toasted pecan halves, roughly chopped
6 tablespoons extra-virgin olive oil
2 tablespoons fresh lemon juice (from 1 lemon)
Kosher salt and black pepper

1 Microwave vinegar in a small microwavable bowl on HIGH until very hot, about 1 minute. Add raisins, stirring to combine. Let stand until raisins are plump, about 10 minutes.

2 Working in batches, roll several kale leaves together into a log shape; thinly slice crosswise into ribbons, and place in a large bowl. Add plumped raisins and any remaining vinegar, cheese, pecans, oil, lemon juice, and desired amount of salt and pepper; toss to coat. Let salad stand 10 minutes before serving.

Crab Cakes

Light, fresh, and generous with the crabmeat. These crab cakes do not disappoint. Celery lends a nice crunch while the panko gives the cakes texture and helps to create a nice golden brown crust.

1 Stir together crushed crackers, eggs, celery, mayonnaise, chives, mustard, Old Bay, salt, and pepper in a large bowl until blended. Carefully fold in crab without breaking up chunks.

2 Shape crab mixture into 12 (3-inch) patties (¾ inch thick) (about ½ cup crab mixture for each). Dredge patties in panko. Preheat oven to 300°F; line a baking sheet with parchment paper.

3 Heat 2 tablespoons oil in a large nonstick skillet over medium. Add 4 patties to hot oil in skillet, and cook until golden brown, about 4 minutes per side. Transfer crab cakes to prepared baking sheet, and place in preheated oven to keep warm. Repeat procedure twice with remaining oil and crab cakes. Serve with Pimiento Rémoulade.

Pimiento Rémoulade

Stir together in a small bowl 1 cup mayonnaise, 2 tablespoons Dijon mustard, 2 tablespoons chopped non-pareil capers, 1 (4-ounce) jar diced pimientos (drained), 2 tablespoons chopped scallions (white and light green parts only from 1 scallion), 2 teaspoons hot sauce (such as Tabasco), 1 teaspoon fresh lemon juice (from 1 lemon), ¼ teaspoon smoked paprika, and ¼ teaspoon black pepper. Cover and refrigerate until ready to serve. Store in an airtight container in refrigerator for up to 3 days. MAKES 1 ³/₄ CUPS

SERVES **12**
HANDS-ON **30 MINUTES**
TOTAL **45 MINUTES,**
INCLUDING RÉMOULADE

---

2 cups hand-crushed saltine crackers (about 1 sleeve)

3 large eggs, lightly beaten

¹/₂ cup finely chopped celery (from 3 stalks)

¹/₃ cup mayonnaise

¹/₄ cup chopped fresh chives

1 tablespoon Dijon mustard

1 teaspoon Old Bay seasoning

³/₄ teaspoon kosher salt

¹/₄ teaspoon black pepper

2 pounds fresh lump crabmeat, drained and picked over

³/₄ cup panko (Japanese-style breadcrumbs)

6 tablespoons canola oil

Pimiento Rémoulade (at left)

Vanilla Bean Pots de Crème

SERVES **12** HANDS-ON **20 MINUTES**
TOTAL **5 HOURS, INCLUDING 4 HOURS CHILLING**

This is a nice, light dessert for a luncheon. Be careful when melting white chocolate as it has a tendency to seize when it gets too hot. Don't let the heavy cream overheat or a large white chocolate ball will be the result.

4 ¼ cups heavy cream
4 ounces white chocolate baking bar, chopped
1 cup whole milk
½ teaspoon kosher salt
1 vanilla bean pod, split lengthwise
9 large egg yolks
½ cup granulated sugar
Sweetened whipped cream
Fresh raspberries

1 Preheat oven to 300°F. Place 12 (4-ounce) ramekins in a large roasting pan.

2 Microwave ¼ cup of the cream in a medium-size microwavable bowl on HIGH until very hot, about 1 minute. Add white chocolate, and stir until melted and smooth. Pour 1 tablespoon white chocolate mixture into each ramekin; set aside.

3 Combine milk, salt, and remaining 4 cups cream in a medium saucepan. Scrape seeds from vanilla bean into cream mixture in saucepan, and add bean pod halves. Bring to a simmer over medium-high, stirring occasionally, 7 to 8 minutes. Remove from heat, cover, and let stand 10 minutes. Discard vanilla bean pod.

4 Place egg yolks and sugar in a large bowl, and whisk vigorously until pale yellow in color, about 4 minutes. Gradually whisk in hot cream mixture until smooth. Pour through a fine wire-mesh strainer, discarding any solids. Pour cream mixture evenly into ramekins in roasting pan. Place roasting pan in preheated oven, and carefully pour hot water into roasting pan until water comes halfway up sides of ramekins.

5 Bake until set around the edges but still wobbly in the center, 45 to 50 minutes. Let cool in water bath 5 minutes. Transfer ramekins to a wire rack, and let cool completely, about 1 hour. Chill until cold, at least 4 hours or up to overnight.

6 Serve the Pots de Crème topped with whipped cream and fresh raspberries.

Chocolate-Dipped Tuile Cookies

MAKES **24** COOKIES HANDS-ON **35 MINUTES**
TOTAL **1 HOUR**

Delicate, crunchy, and buttery, tuiles are a fantastic accompaniment to creamy, custard desserts. The chocolate and pecans give these tuiles a nice festive look and Southern taste.

½ cup (2 ⅛ ounces) sifted unbleached cake flour
½ cup granulated sugar
⅛ teaspoon kosher salt
2 large egg whites
1 teaspoon vanilla extract
¼ cup unsalted butter, melted
4 ounces semisweet chocolate, chopped
½ cup toasted pecan halves, finely chopped

1 Stir together flour, sugar, and salt in a large bowl until combined. Whisk in egg whites and vanilla until blended. Whisk in melted butter until a thin, smooth batter is formed. Cover and refrigerate for 30 minutes.

2 Preheat oven to 350°F. Line a large rimmed baking sheet with a silicone baking mat (such as Silpat).

3 Spoon batter by ½ tablespoonfuls onto prepared baking sheet (3 cookies per sheet), and spread each dollop of batter into a 4-inch thin circle using an offset spatula. Bake in preheated oven until light golden around edges, about 8 to 9 minutes. Let cool on baking sheet for 30 seconds. Working quickly with 1 at a time, carefully remove warm cookies from baking sheet, rolling each around the handle of a wooden spoon to create a cigar-like shape; immediately remove spoon. Repeat procedure 7 times with remaining batter. Cool completely.

4 Microwave chocolate in a medium-size microwavable bowl on HIGH until chocolate is melted, about 2 minutes, stopping to stir every 20 seconds. Dip 1 end of each cooled cookie in melted chocolate, and sprinkle with pecans. Let stand on a wire rack until chocolate is set. Store in an airtight container 8 to 10 days.

CHEERS
to the
SEASON

RAISE A GLASS AND RING IN THE HOLIDAYS WITH A MERRY MASH-UP OF SOUTHERN STANDARDS AND INVENTIVE BITES DESTINED TO BECOME NEW FAVORITES. ONE- AND TWO-BITE APPETIZERS ARE IDEAL COCKTAIL PARTY NIBBLES FOR COME-AND-GO GUESTS, WHILE A SAMPLING OF EVERYTHING CAN MAKE IT A MEAL FOR THOSE WHO DON'T WANT THE GOOD TIME TO END.

THE MENU
SERVES 10 to 12

Red Hot Cranberry-Apple Punch

Southern Potstickers

Egg Salad Deviled Eggs

Andouille-Crawfish Dip

Oatmeal Stout, Fontina, and Pecan Cheese Ball

Greek Wings and Tzatziki Sauce

Hasselback Potato Bites with Feta and Harissa Aïoli

Salted Caramel-Peanut Saltine Brittle

Classic with a Twist

A garden urn brimming with evergreen boughs, ornaments, and a spray of ilex berries (at left) is a striking focal point. Across the room, a lush conifer wreath accented with ribbon, hypericum, and holly berries complements the look.

Draw Them In

A roaring fire, cozy seating, and vibrant accents—fabulous art, shiny objects, cheerful stockings, and a thick evergreen garland draping the mantel—beckon guests to come in, raise a glass, and sit a spell.

Get the Look

Red and green is a Christmas classic freshened up by using a range of each color's hues. A self-service bar station enlists red leather pencil holders to corral bar tools. Trays, ready for service, are a gleaming backdrop for pretty decanters. An open-wire, brass tray collects gifts from guests or parting favors. A natural wreath form is filled with moss, red berries, and glittering stars. Beautiful swirling glass sculptures, used in a novel way here, give this centerpiece bold impact. A striking bouquet of tulips, ranunculus, berries, and greenery spills from a hammered brass pitcher (at right).

Red Hot Cranberry-Apple Punch

SERVES **12 TO 14** HANDS-ON **10 MINUTES**
TOTAL **10 MINUTES**

Cinnamon whisky and ginger liqueur give this punch a kick that recalls the tiny red cinnamon candies used to candy apples.

5 cups cranberry-apple juice drink
1 ½ cups (12 ounces) cinnamon whisky (such as Fireball) liquor
¾ cup (6 ounces) brandy
½ cup (4 ounces) ginger liqueur (such as Domaine de Canton)
6 tablespoons fresh lemon juice (from 1 lemon)
1 Honeycrisp apple, thinly sliced
1 cup frozen whole cranberries
1 (25.4-ounce) bottle sparkling apple cider (such as Martinelli's)

In a large pitcher or a punch bowl, combine juice, whisky, brandy, ginger liqueur, and lemon juice. Refrigerate until ready to serve. To serve, add apple slices and frozen cranberries to juice mixture, and top with sparkling cider. Serve over ice.

VARIATION

Red Hot Cranberry-Apple Mocktail

Combine **1 cup granulated sugar**, **¼ cup water**, **2 cinnamon sticks**, and **2 tablespoons chopped fresh ginger** in a saucepan. Bring to a boil over medium-high; remove from heat, and let cool to room temperature, about 40 minutes. Pour through a wire-mesh strainer into a large pitcher, discarding solids. Stir in **6 cups cranberry-apple juice drink** (such as Ocean Spray Cran-Apple) and **1 cup fresh lemon juice** (from 4 lemons). Refrigerate until ready to serve. To serve, add **1 thinly sliced Honeycrisp apple** and **1 cup frozen whole cranberries**; top with **1 (25.4-ounce) bottle sparkling apple cider** (such as Martinelli's). Serve over ice. SERVES **12**

Southern Potstickers

SERVES **10** HANDS-ON **45 MINUTES** TOTAL **45 MINUTES**

All your Southern barbecue joint favorites collide in this two-bite appetizer with creamy Alabama-style white sauce for dunking.

½ pound shredded or chopped smoked pork
7 tablespoons canola oil
2 cups finely chopped, stemmed collard greens
1 tablespoon chopped garlic (about 3 cloves)
1 tablespoon hot sauce
1 large egg, beaten
½ teaspoon kosher salt
½ teaspoon black pepper
1 (12-ounce) package gyoza wrappers
¾ cup mayonnaise
3 tablespoons apple cider vinegar
½ teaspoon smoked paprika
1 ½ teaspoons honey
½ teaspoon dry mustard
¼ teaspoon cayenne pepper
1 ½ cups water
2 tablespoons chopped scallions

1 Pulse pork in a food processor 10 times until finely chopped. Heat 1 tablespoon of the oil in a large skillet over medium-high. Add the collards, and cook, stirring often, until wilted, 2 minutes. Add garlic; cook, stirring, 1 minute. Remove from heat. Let cool slightly, about 5 minutes. Combine pork, collards, hot sauce, egg, salt, and black pepper in a large bowl.

2 Place gyoza wrappers under a damp towel on a work surface next to a small bowl of water. Working with 1 wrapper at a time, spoon 1 ½ teaspoons pork into center. Use moistened fingertips to coat outside edge of half of wrapper. Fold moistened half over filling. Seal to dry edge, using fingertips to form tiny pleats at edge. Place potsticker, seam side up, on a rimmed baking sheet lined with parchment paper. Press lightly to flatten filling side so potstickers stand seam side up. Cover with a damp towel. Repeat with remaining wrappers and filling to form 30 potstickers.

3 Stir together mayonnaise, vinegar, paprika, honey, dry mustard, and cayenne. Set sauce aside.

4 Heat 2 tablespoons of the oil in a large lidded skillet over medium-high. Add 10 pot stickers, seam side up. Cook until bottoms are light golden brown, 2 to 3 minutes. Add ¼ cup of the water and shake to loosen potstickers. Cover; cook until most water has evaporated and bottoms of potstickers are golden and crispy, 5 to 7 minutes. Uncover; cook until water has evaporated, 1 to 2 minutes. Shake to loosen potstickers. Place a large plate over skillet. Use pot holders to invert skillet over plate, transferring potstickers to plate. Repeat process for remaining potstickers. Sprinkle scallions over potstickers, and serve warm with sauce.

Egg Salad Deviled Eggs

SERVES **12**
HANDS-ON **30 MINUTES**
TOTAL **45 MINUTES**

2 thick-cut bacon slices, each cut into 6 pieces

8 large eggs

½ cup finely chopped arugula

¼ cup mayonnaise

2 tablespoons finely chopped shallot (about 1 medium shallot)

2 tablespoons finely chopped drained capers

1 teaspoon tarragon vinegar

¼ teaspoon kosher salt

¼ teaspoon coarsely ground black pepper

12 thin slices red bell pepper (optional)

The ladies' luncheon egg salad sandwich is ubiquitous for a reason—it's delicious! We figured it was time to put the egg salad back in the egg for a devilishly delicious spin on the drugstore counter classic.

1 Cook bacon in a skillet over medium-high until crisp, 6 to 8 minutes, turning often to brown evenly. Drain on a plate lined with paper towels.

2 Place eggs in a saucepan, and add cold water to cover. Bring to a boil over high. Reduce heat to medium-low, and simmer 10 minutes. Drain and immediately place eggs in a bowl of ice water to cool, about 4 minutes. Peel eggs, and cut in half. Remove the yolks; transfer to a medium bowl, reserving egg white halves. Crumble yolks. Place 12 of the reserved egg white halves on a platter. Finely chop remaining 4 egg white halves, and add to crumbled yolks in bowl. Add arugula, mayonnaise, shallot, capers, vinegar, and salt, stirring gently to combine ingredients.

3 Spoon or pipe mixture generously into egg white halves on platter. Sprinkle with black pepper, and top each with a bacon piece and, if desired, a red pepper slice. Chill until ready to serve.

Divine Ways with Deviled Eggs

Try these innovative ingredient combos for tasty twists on the picnic favorite. Just mix the ingredients below into 12 hard-cooked egg yolks that have been mashed with ⅓ cup plain Greek yogurt, 2 tablespoons mayonnaise, and 1 teaspoon Dijon mustard.

RAGIN' CAJUN
½ cup finely chopped cooked shrimp, 3 Tbsp. sautéed chopped green bell pepper, 1 minced green onion, ¼ tsp. Cajun seasoning, ¼ tsp. hot sauce. Top with cooked shrimp.

TEXAS CAVIAR
3 Tbsp. chopped roasted red bell pepper, 1 minced green onion, 1 Tbsp. minced pickled jalapeño pepper, 1 Tbsp. chopped fresh cilantro, 1 tsp. Italian dressing mix. Top with canned black-eyed peas and fresh cilantro leaves.

DEBUTANTE DEVILS
½ cup cooked fresh lump crabmeat, 2 tsp. fresh tarragon, ½ tsp. lemon zest, ¼ tsp. pepper. Top with cooked fresh crabmeat and watercress.

JUST PEACHY
3 Tbsp. peach preserves, ¼ cup finely chopped country ham, 1 tsp. grated Vidalia onion, ½ tsp. apple cider vinegar, ¼ tsp. pepper. Top with sliced fresh peaches and chopped toasted pecans.

PETER PIPER'S PICK
3 Tbsp. chopped bread-and-butter pickles, 2 Tbsp. chopped capers. Top with pickled okra slices.

Andouille–Crawfish Dip

SERVES **10 TO 12** HANDS-ON **30 MINUTES**
TOTAL **1 HOUR**

Bold bayou flavors meld in this addictive dip.

1 tablespoon canola oil

4 ounces raw andouille sausage, casings removed

1 cup finely diced yellow onion

½ cup finely diced celery

¼ cup finely diced red bell pepper

¼ cup finely diced green bell pepper

2 tablespoons chopped garlic (about 6 medium cloves)

2 teaspoons Old Bay seasoning

½ teaspoon kosher salt

½ teaspoon black pepper

1 (1-pound) package frozen peeled cooked crawfish tails, thawed (reserve any liquid)

8 ounces cream cheese, softened

4 ounces sharp white Cheddar cheese, grated (about 1 cup)

4 ounces pepper Jack cheese, grated (about 1 cup)

2 tablespoons Dijon mustard

2 tablespoons hot sauce

2 tablespoons fresh lemon juice

2 tablespoons chopped fresh parsley

2 tablespoons salted butter, melted

1 cup saltine cracker crumbs (about 20 crackers)

¼ cup thinly sliced scallions

Saltine crackers

1 Preheat oven to 375°F. Lightly grease a 2-quart baking dish. Heat oil in a large skillet over medium-high; add sausage, and cook, stirring to break sausage into small pieces, until completely cooked, about 4 minutes. Add onion, celery, bell peppers, garlic, Old Bay, salt, and black pepper; cook, stirring often, until vegetables are slightly tender, about 6 minutes. Add crawfish tail meat and any liquid from package, and cook, stirring often, until most of the liquid has evaporated, about 2 minutes. Remove from heat.

2 Stir together cream cheese, grated cheeses, mustard, and hot sauce in a medium bowl. Add crawfish mixture, lemon juice, and parsley, and stir until well blended. Transfer mixture to prepared baking dish.

3 In a small bowl, stir together melted butter and cracker crumbs until coated. Sprinkle cracker crumb mixture evenly over crawfish mixture. Bake in preheated oven until dip is hot and bubbly and topping is golden brown, 25 to 30 minutes. Sprinkle with scallions, and serve with saltine crackers.

Oatmeal Stout, Fontina, and Pecan Cheese Ball

SERVES **10** HANDS-ON **20 MINUTES**
TOTAL **2 HOURS, 20 MINUTES, INCLUDING 2 HOURS CHILLING**

Beer cheese is a German biergarten staple, often served with rye or pumpernickel bread and pretzels.

2 tablespoons salted butter

¼ cup chopped shallots (from 1 shallot)

⅓ cup oatmeal stout beer (such as Anderson Valley Barney Flats)

1 (8-ounce) package cream cheese, softened

8 ounces fontina cheese, grated (about 2 cups)

2 tablespoons chopped fresh flat-leaf parsley

1 tablespoon Dijon mustard

½ teaspoon kosher salt

½ teaspoon black pepper

½ cup chopped toasted pecans

Pretzel rods

1 Melt butter in a saucepan over medium. Add shallots, and cook, stirring often, until shallots are softened, 3 to 4 minutes. Add beer, and bring to a simmer over medium-high. Reduce the heat to medium, and cook until liquid is reduced to about 3 tablespoons, about 8 minutes. Let cool slightly, about 15 minutes.

2 Stir together cream cheese, fontina cheese, parsley, mustard, salt, pepper, and cooled shallot mixture in a medium bowl until well blended. (Cover and refrigerate cheese mixture for 30 minutes if not firm enough to form into a ball.) Shape mixture into bite-size balls, cover, and refrigerate 2 hours.

3 Just before serving, roll cheese balls in chopped toasted pecans to completely coat outside of balls. Insert a pretzel rod in each for easy pick up.

Greek Wings and Tzatziki Sauce

SERVES **10** HANDS-ON **30 MINUTES** TOTAL **1 HOUR**

The usual game day wings go Greek with a refreshing creamy cucumber sauce for dipping.

GREEK LEMON-PEPPER WINGS
4 pounds chicken wings, patted dry and cut at joints, wing tips discarded
¼ cup olive oil
1 tablespoon kosher salt
3 tablespoons salted butter
1 tablespoon lemon zest, plus 2 tablespoons fresh juice
2 tablespoons chopped garlic (about 6 cloves)
1 tablespoon honey
2 teaspoons black pepper
1 teaspoon chopped fresh oregano

TZATZIKI SAUCE
1 cup grated English cucumber
1 cup whole-milk plain Greek yogurt
¼ cup olive oil
¼ cup chopped fresh flat-leaf parsley
1 teaspoon lemon zest, plus 2 tablespoons fresh juice
1 teaspoon chopped garlic (about 1 clove)
1 teaspoon kosher salt
¼ teaspoon cayenne pepper

ADDITIONAL INGREDIENTS
Assorted crudités

1 Prepare the Wings: Preheat oven to 400°F. Line a rimmed baking sheet with aluminum foil. Set a wire rack on prepared baking sheet; coat rack with cooking spray. In a large bowl, toss wings with olive oil and 2 teaspoons of the salt. Place wings in a single layer on rack without touching. Bake until cooked through and skin is golden (will not be crispy), about 45 minutes. Increase oven temperature to a broil with rack set 6 inches from heat.

2 Combine butter, lemon zest and juice, garlic, honey, pepper, oregano, and remaining 1 teaspoon salt in a small saucepan. Cook over medium, stirring, until butter is melted and honey is dissolved, about 2 minutes. Remove from heat.

3 Prepare the Tzatziki Sauce: Stir together cucumber, yogurt, olive oil, chopped parsley, lemon zest and juice, garlic, salt, and cayenne in a medium bowl. Refrigerate until ready to use.

4 Transfer wings to a clean large bowl. Drizzle butter mixture over wings; toss to coat. Return wings to rack, and broil in preheated oven until browned and lightly crisp, about 1 minute per side.

5 To serve, arrange crudités on half of a large platter, place Tzatziki Sauce in a bowl in center, and arrange wings on other side of platter; serve immediately.

Hasselback Potato Bites with Feta and Harissa Aïoli

SERVES **12** HANDS-ON **15 MINUTES** TOTAL **1 HOUR**

The humble potato wows when dressed with zesty harissa and crumbled feta.

12 (2 ½-ounce) small Yukon Gold potatoes
¼ cup (2 ounces) salted butter, melted
1 tablespoon chopped fresh thyme leaves
1 ½ teaspoons kosher salt
¼ cup mayonnaise
3 tablespoons harissa
1 tablespoon fresh lemon juice (from 1 lemon)
¼ cup crumbled feta cheese
2 tablespoons chopped fresh chives

1 Preheat oven to 425°F. Line a rimmed baking sheet with aluminum foil.

2 Slice each potato crosswise in ⅛-inch intervals, cutting to within ¼ inch of the bottom of the potato, leaving bottom of potato intact. Arrange potatoes, cut sides up, on prepared baking sheet.

3 Stir together butter, thyme, and 1 teaspoon of the salt in a small bowl. Spoon mixture evenly over potatoes, being sure to get butter into cuts. Bake in preheated oven until potatoes are tender and outsides are golden and slightly crispy, about 45 minutes.

4 Meanwhile, stir together mayonnaise, harissa, lemon juice, and remaining ½ teaspoon salt in a small bowl until blended. Place baked potatoes on a platter; drizzle with mayonnaise mixture, and sprinkle with feta and chives. Serve hot or at room temperature.

Salted Caramel–Peanut Saltine Brittle

SERVES 20 TO 22 HANDS-ON **20 MINUTES**
TOTAL **1 HOUR, 40 MINUTES**

Make enough for your guests to enjoy and to take home as a party favor.

40 saltine crackers (from 1 ½ sleeves)
1 cup (8 ounces) unsalted butter, cubed
1 cup packed light brown sugar
1 ½ cups chopped unsalted roasted peanuts
1 (4-ounce) bittersweet chocolate baking bar, chopped
1 teaspoon flaky sea salt (such as Maldon)

1 Preheat oven to 350°F. Line a 15- x 10-inch jelly-roll pan with aluminum foil; lightly grease foil. Arrange crackers in a single layer on bottom of pan.

2 In a large saucepan, melt butter over medium-high. Whisk in brown sugar, and cook, whisking often, until mixture comes to a boil. Continue cooking, gently whisking often, until fully melted and bubbly, about 3 minutes. Remove from heat, and pour evenly over crackers, spreading mixture to cover crackers completely. Bake in preheated oven until bubbly, about 8 minutes. Remove from oven, and immediately sprinkle chopped peanuts evenly over crackers, pressing to adhere. Let cool 20 minutes.

3 Microwave chocolate in a microwavable container on HIGH until chocolate is melted, about 1 ½ minutes, stirring every 30 seconds. Drizzle melted chocolate over cooled crackers, and sprinkle with flaky sea salt. Refrigerate, uncovered, on jelly-roll pan until set, about 1 hour. Break into pieces, and serve on a platter. Store in an airtight container in a cool place up to 1 week.

VARIATION

Rosemary-Cashew Cracker Brittle

SERVES 20 TO 22 HANDS-ON **20 MINUTES**
TOTAL **40 MINUTES**

Omit chocolate. Substitute **1 (5.5-ounce) package multigrain flax seeded flatbread crackers** (such as Back to Nature) for saltines and **1 ½ cups cashews** for peanuts. Prepare recipe as directed, immediately sprinkling **1 tablespoon chopped fresh rosemary** over crackers after baking. Top with cashews and sea salt, and let cool 20 minutes. Break into pieces, and serve on a platter. Store in an airtight container in a cool place up to 1 week.

Visions of SUGARPLUMS

DON'T RELEGATE SUGARPLUMS TO 'TWAS-THE-NIGHT-BEFORE-
CHRISTMAS DREAMS. HOST AN UNFORGETTABLE DESSERT PARTY
OPEN HOUSE THIS HOLIDAY SEASON AND WHIP UP A KALEIDOSCOPE
OF SWEET TREATS TO SHARE WITH FAMILY AND FRIENDS.

THE MENU
SERVES 8 to 10

Steaming Eggnog Mochas

Dark Chocolate and Peppermint Bark

Christmas Sprinkle Truffle Balls

White Chocolate-Dipped Turtle Candy

Eggnog Buckeyes

Green Swirl Meringue Kisses

Red Turkish Delight Candy

Peanut Butter Patties

Coconut Thumbprint Cookies with Key Lime Curd

Butterscotch Pie Bars

Pistachio Nougat

Baubles & Blossoms

Mesh cones hold glorious sprays of flowers, berries, branches, and dyed moss, brightening the staircase with a dramatic dose of color (below). A towering display of peonies, heather, amaranth, and roses stands at attention beneath an ornament-embellished chandelier.

Glam It Up!

Subdued is nice. Traditional is fine. But drama is divine! Blushing poinsettias blaze against a lacy garland of green. Mohair stockings in jewel tones play well with the abstract art and bold pillows.

Get the Look

Gradations of purple, red, and pink are striking complements to green boughs and tender leaves. The palette is fitting for the holidays. Handsome containers, clean architectural lines, and simplicity keep things fresh and inviting without being overly feminine. Guests can help themselves to foil-wrapped chocolates secured to a Styrofoam tree form. At right, the open space between boughs of a tiny red fir give it a modern feel. It's a fun tree variety to decorate too. Ornaments shine in the negative space between the branches. Here, they also serve as a "mulch" topper to a glimmering gold planter.

Steaming Eggnog Mochas

Better than a gourmet coffee from your local barista. Make sure you stir enough so that milk doesn't scorch on the bottom of the pan. Eggnog is a seasonal find in grocery stores, and it's available on amazon.com in a shelf-stable form from Borden dairy.

1 Stir together chocolate milk, eggnog, coffee, and 1 cup of the heavy cream in a large saucepan. Cook over medium-low, stirring often, until hot. Remove from heat, and stir in vanilla.

2 Beat remaining 1 cup heavy cream in a medium bowl with an electric mixer on high speed until stiff peaks form. Serve eggnog mixture in cups with a dollop of whipped cream. Garnish with ground nutmeg and shaved chocolate.

SERVES **10**
HANDS-ON **15 MINUTES**
TOTAL **15 MINUTES**

4 cups whole chocolate milk
4 cups refrigerated eggnog
1 cup very strong brewed coffee
2 cups heavy cream
1 teaspoon vanilla extract
Ground nutmeg
Shaved bittersweet chocolate

Dark Chocolate and Peppermint Bark

MAKES **16 PIECES** HANDS-ON **10 MINUTES**
TOTAL **4 HOURS, 10 MINUTES, INCLUDING 4 HOURS COOLING**

This bark is so simple to make with just two ingredients. Even better, you can get creative and add other toppings that go well with dark chocolate. Try adding crumbled pretzels, saltines, or popcorn for a savory element, or add in your favorite candies or nuts. This is a great bark basic to build upon.

1 pound bittersweet chocolate bars	**1 pound hard peppermint candies or candy canes**

1 Line a 15- x 10-inch jelly-roll pan with parchment paper. Chop chocolate, and place in a large microwavable bowl.

2 Place peppermint or candy canes in a large ziplock plastic freezer bag; crush candy with a mallet or rolling pin, leaving some pieces larger than others.

3 Microwave chocolate on MEDIUM (50% power) until melted and smooth, 1 ½ to 2 minutes, stirring at 30-second intervals.

4 Transfer 1 cup crushed peppermint to a fine wire-mesh strainer; hold strainer over melted chocolate, and tap side of strainer to sift fine peppermint dust into chocolate. Reserve 1 cup candy in strainer. Stir remaining crushed peppermint into chocolate mixture.

5 Using a flexible spatula, spoon chocolate mixture onto prepared jelly-roll pan, and spread to ¼-inch thickness. Sprinkle with reserved candy from strainer, gently pressing candy into chocolate.

6 Let cool at room temperature until completely firm, about 4 hours or overnight. Break or cut bark into 16 pieces. Store in an airtight container in a cool place up to 2 weeks.

VARIATION

Mississippi Mud Chocolate Bark

Omit peppermint candies. Prepare recipe as directed, omitting Steps 2 and 4 and sprinkling chocolate with **1 cup each miniature marshmallows** and **coarsely chopped toasted pecans** in Step 5.

Christmas Sprinkle Truffle Balls

MAKES **ABOUT 2 ½ DOZEN** HANDS-ON **20 MINUTES**
TOTAL **15 HOURS, 20 MINUTES, INCLUDING 15 HOURS CHILLING**

These sweet little morsels are a great treat to make with kids. They can roll the truffle balls and coat them with sprinkles. Place the sprinkles in individual small bowls to keep things neat and rolling easy.

1 ½ (4-ounce) white chocolate baking bars, melted according to package directions	**¾ cup crushed shortbread cookies (such as Walkers or Lorna Doone)**
1 (8-ounce) package cream cheese, softened	**2 teaspoons heavy cream**
	1 teaspoon vanilla extract
	⅛ teaspoon kosher salt
	1 cup assorted Christmas candy sprinkles

1 Combine melted chocolate and softened cream cheese in bowl of a heavy-duty stand mixer fitted with paddle attachment; beat on medium speed until smooth. Add cookies, cream, vanilla, and salt, beating just until blended. Spoon mixture into a glass bowl; cover and chill 2 hours.

2 Shape the mixture into 1-inch balls and place in a single layer on a parchment paper-lined rimmed baking sheet. Cover and chill 12 hours or overnight. Roll balls in Christmas candy sprinkles; chill 1 hour before serving. Store in an airtight container in refrigerator up to 5 days.

White Chocolate-Dipped Turtle Candy

After the last gift is opened and last guest has gone, if you have some leftovers, you can chop them up and freeze them to add on top of ice cream or to whirl into a milkshake for a treat anytime of the year.

MAKES 2 DOZEN
HANDS-ON 40 MINUTES
TOTAL 1 HOUR, 10 MINUTES

1 Cook caramels, butter, and water in a heavy saucepan over low, stirring constantly, until smooth, about 15 minutes. Stir in pecans. Remove from heat; cool in pan 5 minutes.

2 Spoon caramel mixture (2 tablespoons per candy) 1 ½ inches apart onto a parchment paper-lined rimmed baking sheet. Freeze 30 minutes.

3 Meanwhile, microwave candy coating, white chocolate, and shortening in a large microwavable bowl on MEDIUM (50% power) 1 minute; stir mixture, and continue microwaving until melted and smooth, about 1 ½ more minutes, stirring at 30-second intervals. Dip frozen candies in white chocolate mixture, allowing excess white chocolate mixture to drip off; place on lightly greased wax paper. Quickly sprinkle tops with coarse sea salt, if desired. Chill until firm, about 30 minutes. Store in an airtight container in refrigerator up to 7 days.

1 (14-ounce) package caramel candies

2 tablespoons salted butter

2 tablespoons water

3 cups toasted pecan halves and pieces

1 (1-pound) package vanilla candy coating

2 (4-ounce) white chocolate baking bars, chopped

2 tablespoons vegetable shortening

Coarse sea salt (optional)

Eggnog Buckeyes

MAKES **4 DOZEN** HANDS-ON **30 MINUTES** TOTAL **1 HOUR**

Creamy and smooth, the nutmeg-spiked flavors of eggnog shine through in this rich cookie.

1 cup smooth cookie butter (such as Speculoos)
½ cup (4 ounces) unsalted butter, softened
3 cups (about 12 ounces) powdered sugar
1 tablespoon (½ ounce) bourbon
½ teaspoon grated fresh nutmeg
3 (4-ounce) bittersweet baking chocolate bars, chopped

1 Combine cookie butter and butter in bowl of a heavy-duty stand mixer fitted with paddle attachment; beat on low speed until creamy and smooth. Gradually add powdered sugar, ¼ cup at a time, beating just until combined after each addition. Add bourbon and nutmeg, and beat on medium speed until creamy and smooth.

2 Shape mixture into 48 (1 tablespoon) balls, and place cookie balls on a parchment paper-lined baking sheet. Freeze for 30 minutes.

3 Meanwhile, microwave chocolate in a small microwavable bowl on MEDIUM (50% power) until chocolate is melted and smooth, about 2 minutes, stirring at 30-second intervals. Using a toothpick or candy dipper, dip bottom two-thirds of each cookie ball into melted chocolate, and return to parchment paper-lined baking sheet. Refrigerate 1 hour before serving. Store between layers of wax paper in an airtight container in refrigerator up to 1 week.

Green Swirl Meringue Kisses

MAKES **2 DOZEN** HANDS-ON **15 MINUTES** TOTAL **5 HOURS, 15 MINUTES, INCLUDING 3 HOURS COOLING**

Meringue cookies are easy and beautiful and especially festive when made into fun green swirls.

6 large egg whites
1 ½ teaspoons white vinegar
1 ½ cups granulated sugar
1 teaspoon vanilla extract
Green food coloring gel

1 Preheat oven to 200°F. Place egg whites in the bowl of a heavy-duty stand mixer fitted with whisk attachment, and let stand at room temperature 20 minutes. Beat egg whites on high speed until stiff peaks form. Reduce speed to medium, and add vinegar. Gradually add sugar, ¼ cup at a time, beating just until blended after each addition. Beat 2 minutes. Beat in vanilla.

2 Fit a large decorating bag with a star tip. Using green food coloring gel, paint 3 or 4 evenly spaced thin stripes on inside of bag, starting at tip end and ending three-fourths of the way up bag. Gently spoon egg white mixture into center of bag, filling three-fourths full, setting remaining egg white mixture aside. Pipe egg white mixture into 2-inch-wide swirl shapes (about 2 tablespoons each) onto parchment paper-lined baking sheets, leaving 1 inch between meringues. Repeat with remaining egg white mixture, using a clean decorating bag for each batch. (Each swirl should be formed in one fluid movement.)

3 Bake in preheated oven until completely firm and stiff to the touch, about 2 hours. Turn off oven, but do not open door; let meringues stand in oven, with door closed, until completely cool, about 3 hours. Store in an airtight container at room temperature up to 5 days.

Red Turkish Delight Candy

MAKES **3 DOZEN** HANDS-ON **1 HOUR** TOTAL **5 HOURS, INCLUDING 4 HOURS TO SET**

This is a very old-fashioned recipe (perhaps older than Grandma's fruitcake!) with a gelatinlike consistency.

1 ⅔ cups granulated sugar
2 tablespoons fresh lemon juice (from 1 lemon)
2 cups plus 2 tablespoons tap water
½ cup plus 2 tablespoons cornstarch
4 (1-ounce) envelopes unflavored gelatin
¼ cup powdered sugar
1 teaspoon bottled rose water
½ cup coarsely chopped toasted blanched almonds
4 drops of red gel paste food color (such as AmeriColor Red Red)

1 Stir together granulated sugar, lemon juice, and 1 ¼ cups of the tap water in a medium-size heavy saucepan. Cook over low, stirring occasionally, until sugar dissolves, about 8 minutes. Bring mixture to a simmer over medium.

2 Whisk together ½ cup of the cornstarch and remaining ¾ cup plus 2 tablespoons tap water in a small bowl until smooth; stir in gelatin until combined. Add gelatin mixture to sugar mixture, and cook, stirring constantly, until gelatin dissolves, about 5 minutes. Simmer gently, stirring occasionally, until mixture has thickened, about 20 minutes.

3 Stir together 2 tablespoons of the powdered sugar and the remaining 2 tablespoons cornstarch in a small bowl. Lightly grease an 8-inch square pan, and line with plastic wrap. Lightly dust plastic wrap with powdered sugar mixture, tapping out excess.

4 Remove saucepan from heat. Stir in rose water, almonds, and food coloring. Pour mixture into prepared pan, and level top of mixture with an offset spatula. Let stand at room temperature until completely set, about 4 hours. Cut into 36 squares, and sprinkle with remaining 2 tablespoons powdered sugar. Store in an airtight container at room temperature up to 5 days.

Peanut Butter Patties

SERVES 20 HANDS-ON 40 MINUTES TOTAL 6 HOURS, 10 MINUTES, INCLUDING 4 HOURS, 40 MINUTES CHILLING

These yummy treats are a nice accompaniment to ice cream. Be aware that the peanut butter mixture or peppermint mixture should be frozen onto the cookies before dipping or else they will melt into the chocolate and drip off the sides of the cookies.

1 cup (8 ounces) salted butter, softened
1 ½ cups (about 6 ounces) powdered sugar
2 ½ teaspoons vanilla extract
2 cups (about 8 ½ ounces) all-purpose flour
¼ teaspoon baking powder
⅛ teaspoon table salt
1 ½ cups creamy peanut butter
1 ½ cups semisweet chocolate chips
2 teaspoons canola oil

1 Beat butter in a medium bowl with an electric mixer on medium speed until creamy. Gradually add ¾ cup of the powdered sugar, beating until smooth. Beat in 2 teaspoons of the vanilla until blended.

2 Stir together flour, baking powder, and salt in a medium bowl. Gradually add flour mixture to butter mixture, beating at low speed just until blended after each addition.

3 Shape dough into 2 (8-inch) logs. Wrap each log in wax paper, and refrigerate 4 hours.

4 Preheat oven to 350°F. Cut each log into 20 slices (about ⅓ to ½ inch thick). Place slices 1 inch apart on parchment paper-lined baking sheets.

5 Bake in preheated oven until edges of cookies are golden, 10 to 12 minutes. Transfer cookies from baking sheets to wire racks to cool completely (about 20 minutes).

6 Beat peanut butter and remaining ¾ cup powdered sugar and ½ teaspoon vanilla in a small microwavable bowl with an electric mixer on high speed until very smooth and creamy (mixture will become lighter in color). Microwave peanut butter mixture on HIGH until mixture is very warm, 30 seconds to 1 minute, stirring after 30 seconds.

7 Transfer peanut butter mixture to a large ziplock plastic freezer bag. Snip 1 corner of bag, and pipe dollops of peanut butter filling into the center of each cookie, leaving ¼ to ½ inch around edge. Freeze cookies until peanut butter filling is firm, about 20 minutes.

8 Meanwhile, stir together chocolate chips and oil in a small microwavable bowl. Microwave on HIGH until chocolate is melted and smooth, 30 seconds to 1 minute, stirring after 30 seconds.

9 Place chilled cookies on wire racks set on a rimmed baking sheet. Gently spoon melted chocolate mixture over cookies, covering tops completely. Refrigerate cookies 20 minutes before serving. Store in an airtight container at room temperature up to 10 days.

VARIATION

Peppermint Patties

Omit peanut butter, increase powdered sugar to 2 ¼ cups (about 10 ounces), and reduce vanilla to 2 teaspoons. Prepare recipe as directed through Step 5. Stir together 3 tablespoons softened unsalted butter, **3 teaspoons heavy cream, ¼ teaspoon peppermint extract** and remaining 1 ½ cups powdered sugar in a small bowl until smooth. Proceed with recipe as directed in Steps 7 through 9.

Merry Morsels

Cake stands, a bar caddy, canisters, and cups are all enlisted into service on this sweet sideboard. Varying heights and serving pieces add interest and make navigating the deliciousness easier.

Coconut Thumbprint Cookies with Key Lime Curd

MAKES **3 1/2 DOZEN**
HANDS-ON **55 MINUTES**
TOTAL **6 HOURS, 25 MINUTES,
INCLUDING 4 HOURS CHILLING**

KEY LIME CURD

1 cup granulated sugar

1/4 cup salted butter, softened

2 large eggs, at room
   temperature

1/2 cup bottled Key lime juice
   (such as Nellie & Joe's), at room
   temperature

COOKIES

1 cup sweetened flaked coconut

1 cup (8 ounces) salted butter,
   softened

3/4 cup (about 3 ounces)
   powdered sugar

1/4 cup granulated sugar

1 large egg yolk

1 teaspoon vanilla extract

3 cups (about 12 3/4 ounces)
   all-purpose flour

1/2 teaspoon kosher salt

1/2 teaspoon baking powder

Lime zest

Use any leftover lime curd as a topping for pancakes with fresh berries and powdered sugar on Christmas morning. It also can be used as a spread for biscuits or toast with a steaming mug of tea.

1 Prepare the Key Lime Curd: Beat sugar and butter in a medium bowl with an electric mixer on medium speed until blended. Add eggs, 1 at a time, beating just until blended after each addition. Gradually add Key lime juice to butter mixture, beating at low speed just until blended after each addition. (Mixture may separate at this stage, but will emulsify as it is heated and whisked in Step 2.)

2 Transfer mixture to a heavy 4-quart saucepan. Cook over medium-low, whisking constantly, until mixture thickens and just begins to bubble, 14 to 16 minutes. Remove saucepan from heat, and let mixture cool in saucepan 30 minutes. Transfer mixture to a small bowl, and place heavy-duty plastic wrap directly on surface of warm curd (to prevent a film from forming), and refrigerate until firm, about 4 hours. Store in an airtight container in refrigerator for up to 2 weeks.

3 Prepare the Cookies: Preheat oven to 375°F. Pulse coconut in a food processor until finely chopped, about 10 times. Transfer to a small bowl, and set aside.

4 Beat butter and powdered and granulated sugars in a medium bowl with an electric mixer on medium speed until smooth, about 1 minute. Add egg yolk and vanilla, and beat on low speed just until incorporated. Whisk together flour, salt, and baking powder in a small bowl, and add to butter mixture, beating on low speed just until incorporated after each addition.

5 Scoop dough into 1 tablespoon balls, and roll in finely chopped coconut to coat lightly. Place cookies 1 inch apart on parchment paper-lined baking sheets. Press your thumb or the end of a wooden spoon into each ball, forming an indentation.

6 Bake in preheated oven until cookies are set and coconut is browned, about 13 to 15 minutes. Transfer baking sheets to wire racks, and immediately reshape indentations by pressing again with your thumb or spoon. Transfer cookies to wire racks to cool completely, about 30 minutes.

7 Spoon or pipe about 1/2 teaspoon Key Lime Curd into indentation of each cookie. Garnish with lime zest. Store in an airtight container at room temperature up to 7 days.

Butterscotch Pie Bars

SERVES **10** HANDS-ON **30 MINUTES** TOTAL **3 HOURS, 45 MINUTES, INCLUDING 1 HOUR CHILLING**

A delicious change of pace from the parade of chocolate treats, these pie bars are a nice gift for teachers, coworkers, and friends. The crust may look dry when you are patting it down in the pan, and there may even be some loose bits of flour as well. Don't be deterred. The recipe will come out perfectly even so.

- 2 cups (about 8 ½ ounces) all-purpose flour
- ¾ cup (about 3 ounces) powdered sugar
- ¾ cup (6 ounces) cold salted butter, cubed
- 2 cups butterscotch morsels
- ¾ cup packed light brown sugar
- ¾ cup light corn syrup
- ¼ cup (2 ounces) salted butter, melted
- 2 teaspoons vanilla extract
- ¼ teaspoon table salt
- 3 large eggs, lightly beaten
- 3 cups coarsely chopped toasted pecans
- 1 cup sweetened flaked coconut

1 Preheat oven to 350°F. Line bottom and sides of a 13- x 9-inch pan with heavy-duty aluminum foil, allowing 2 to 3 inches to extend over sides. Lightly grease foil.

2 Pulse flour, powdered sugar, and cubed butter in a food processor until mixture resembles coarse meal, 8 to 9 times. Press mixture on bottom and ¾ inch up sides of prepared pan.

3 Bake in preheated oven 15 minutes. Remove pan from oven, and sprinkle butterscotch morsels over hot crust. Cool completely on a wire rack, about 30 minutes.

4 Whisk together brown sugar, corn syrup, melted butter, vanilla, salt, and eggs in a large bowl until smooth. Stir in toasted pecans and coconut, and spoon into prepared crust.

5 Bake at 350°F until golden and set, 30 to 35 minutes. Cool completely in pan on a wire rack, about 1 hour. Chill 1 hour. Lift baked bars from pan, using foil sides as handles. Transfer to a cutting board; cut into 20 bars. Store in an airtight container at room temperature up to 2 weeks.

Pistachio Nougat

MAKES **3 ½ DOZEN** HANDS-ON **15 MINUTES** TOTAL **2 HOURS, 15 MINUTES, INCLUDING 2 HOURS CHILLING**

Simultaneously soft and crunchy, this nougat was a hit in the Test Kitchen. These are super sweet but light, so you don't feel like you're overindulging if you eat just a few.

- 1 (11-ounce) package white chocolate chips
- 1 (7-ounce) jar marshmallow creme
- ⅔ cup coarsely chopped salted pistachios
- ¼ teaspoon vanilla extract

1 Melt white chocolate chips in a medium bowl according to package directions. Cool 5 minutes. Stir in marshmallow creme, pistachios, and vanilla.

2 Cut 2 sheets of wax paper, each 18 inches long. Divide mixture in half, and place each on bottom one-fourth of a wax paper sheet. Fold bottom edge of wax paper over pistachio mixture to cover, and using wax paper, roll each into a 14- to 16-inch-long log (about ¾ inch in diameter). Wrap each log in wax paper, and refrigerate until firm, about 2 hours. Unwrap logs, and cut each into 1-inch pieces; wrap each piece individually in plastic wrap, colorful cellophane, or wax paper. Store in an airtight container at room temperature up to 5 days.

Sterling TRADITIONS

DRESS THE TABLE FOR THE CLASSIC
CHRISTMAS FEAST WITH HEIRLOOM PIECES
AND COLLECTED FINDS MIXED WITH
MODERN ACCENTS FOR AN ECLECTIC-FORMAL
LOOK THAT IS ANYTHING BUT STUFFY.

THE MENU

SERVES 10

Apple Cider-Champagne
Cocktail

Rustic Celery Root Soup
with Brioche Croutons

Butter Lettuce, Seckel Pear,
and Pecan Salad

Lacquered Satsuma Turkey

Oyster Dressing

Savory Sorghum-Benne-
Sweet Potato Casserole

Blistered Green Beans
with Lemony Breadcrumbs

Fruitcake Trifle with
Bourbon Cream Custard
and Spiced Whipped Cream

Chocolate Pecan Pie

At Your Service

A transferware compote filled with lilies, lisianthus, lamb's ears, and seeded eucalyptus brightens the bar (left). A sterling warming tray glimmers beneath a spray of gunni eucalyptus, succulents, pinecones, and brunia on the coffee table.

Surprise & Delight

A striking parade of opalescent bud vases marches in line with a gunni eucalyptus garland for a bold centerpiece. Mercury glass ornaments, silver goblets, and flatware reflect the light, adding sparkle.

Get the Look

Dark flowers like scabiosa pop against white blooms, like these lilies with bright green centers. It's an eye-catching display on a mantel accented with glittery ornaments and mercury glass trees. Ornaments also line the base of a wispy cypress tree, while a gentle wave of seeded eucalyptus frames fire and front door. Pretty packages repeat the elegant color scheme used throughout. An unexpected backdrop—a gleaming silver tray—is used to highlight the bundle of flowers and greenery that hangs from the knocker of the glossy black front door.

Apple Cider-Champagne Cocktail

Some may think it sacrilege to cut Champagne with apple cider, but the resulting cocktail is a festive sipper.

1 Toss chopped apples, lemon juice, and nutmeg together in a small bowl.

2 Combine chopped apple mixture, cider, and vodka in a cocktail shaker filled with ice. Cover with lid, and shake vigorously until thoroughly chilled, about 30 seconds. Strain into 2 separate ice-filled glasses. Top evenly with Champagne, and garnish with apple wedges or cranberries.

SERVES **2**
HANDS-ON **10 MINUTES**
TOTAL **10 MINUTES**

½ cup chopped Fuji apples

4 teaspoons fresh lemon juice (from 1 lemon)

¼ teaspoon freshly grated nutmeg

¾ cup chilled filtered apple cider

¼ cup (2 ounces) vodka

½ cup (4 ounces) chilled Champagne

Fuji apple wedges or fresh cranberries

Know Your Bubbly

For toasting or cocktails, it helps to know Champagne from Cava and Prosecco from Lambrusco.

ASTI
Sweet, sparkling white wine made from a single tank fermentation of Moscato Bianco (Muscat) grapes in the Italian Piedmont region near the towns of Asti and Alba.

CAVA
Dry to sweet white or rosé sparkling wine produced most commonly in Catalonia, Spain, from Parellada, Xarel-lo or Macabeu grapes.

PROSECCO
Light, sparkling white wine named for the village of Prosecco, where it originated. It is traditionally made from Glera grapes, but other varieties may also be used.

CRÉMANT
Aged, sparkling French white and rosé wines made outside the region of Champagne from handpicked grapes.

LAMBRUSCO
A red wine grape and type of red wine—from dry to sweet—made in the Emilia-Romagna and Lombardy regions of Italy.

FRANCIACORTA
Dry to sweet sparkling white and red wines made from Chardonnay, Pinot Nero, and Pinot Bianco grapes in the province of Brescia (Lombardy) in Italy.

CALIFORNIA SPARKLING WINE
Over 300 producers in the state make sparkling wine, from dry to sweet, primarily made from Chardonnay, Pinot Blanc, and Pinot Noir grapes.

Rustic Celery Root Soup with Brioche Croutons

SERVES **10** HANDS-ON **40 MINUTES** TOTAL **1 HOUR**

Homely celery root is an often overlooked vegetable that deserves attention. This bulbous root of the celery plant has a mild celery flavor and starchy flesh that makes it perfect for soup. Truffle oil and crunchy croutons made from eggy French brioche take this veggie from humble to handsome.

- 8 tablespoons salted butter
- 2 medium leeks (white and light green parts only), thinly sliced (about 3 cups)
- 1 tablespoon chopped fresh thyme
- ½ cup (4 ounces) Madeira
- 3 tablespoons all-purpose flour
- 8 cups chicken stock
- 2½ to 3 pounds celery root, peeled and cubed (9 cups cubes)
- ½ pound peeled cubed Yukon Gold potatoes (about 4 medium)
- 1 teaspoon kosher salt
- ¼ teaspoon white pepper
- 5 ounces brioche, crusts trimmed and cut into ¼-inch cubes
- 8 teaspoons white truffle oil or extra-virgin olive oil
- ¼ cup thinly sliced chives

1 Melt 4 tablespoons of butter in a Dutch oven over medium-high until foamy. Add leeks, and cook, stirring occasionally, 3 minutes. Add thyme, reduce heat to medium, and cook, stirring occasionally, until translucent, 6 to 8 minutes. Add Madeira. Cook on high, stirring occasionally, until liquid is almost evaporated, 3 to 4 minutes.

2 Whisk flour and ½ cup stock in a bowl. Add flour mixture, celery root, potatoes, salt, pepper, and remaining 7 ½ cups stock; stir to combine. Cover. Bring to a boil over high. Reduce heat to medium. Simmer until celery root is tender, about 20 minutes.

3 Transfer one-third of celery root mixture to a blender. Remove center piece of blender lid (to allow steam to escape); secure lid, and place a towel over opening in lid (to prevent splatters). Process until smooth, about 30 seconds. Transfer to a large bowl. Repeat process twice with remaining mixture.

4 Melt remaining 4 tablespoons butter in a large skillet over medium-high. Add brioche cubes, and cook, stirring often, until toasted, about 3 minutes.

5 Ladle soup into bowls. Top with brioche croutons, drizzle evenly with oil, and sprinkle with chives.

Butter Lettuce, Seckel Pear, and Pecan Salad

SERVES **10** HANDS-ON **20 MINUTES**
TOTAL **20 MINUTES**

Tender greens dotted with new-harvest pecans and juicy Seckel pears—a diminutive variety also called "candy pears" for their sweet flesh—make a light and lovely start to the meal.

- 1 large egg white
- 2 cups pecan halves
- 1 teaspoon light brown sugar
- Pinch of cayenne pepper
- 1½ teaspoons kosher salt
- ¼ cup fresh lemon juice (from 1 large lemon)
- ⅓ cup minced shallot (from 1 large shallot)
- 2 teaspoons chopped fresh thyme
- 2 teaspoons honey
- 1 teaspoon Dijon mustard
- ¾ teaspoon black pepper
- ⅔ cup olive oil
- 2 heads butter lettuce, cored and separated into leaves
- 4 Seckel pears, sliced
- 5 ounces Gorgonzola cheese, crumbled (about 1¼ cups)
- ¼ cup sweetened dried cranberries or fresh pomegranate arils

1 Preheat oven to 375°F. Whisk egg white in a small bowl until frothy. Add pecans, brown sugar, cayenne, and ½ teaspoon of the salt, and toss to coat. Arrange pecan mixture in a single layer on a parchment-lined rimmed baking sheet. Bake in the preheated oven until toasted and crispy, about 9 minutes. Cool on baking sheet 10 minutes.

2 Whisk together the lemon juice, shallot, thyme, honey, Dijon, black pepper, and the remaining 1 teaspoon salt in a medium bowl. Gradually drizzle in oil, whisking until blended. Set dressing aside.

3 Arrange lettuce on a platter; top with sliced pears and crumbled cheese. Drizzle with dressing, and sprinkle with toasted pecan mixture and dried cranberries.

Lacquered Satsuma Turkey

SERVES **12**
HANDS-ON **50 MINUTES**
TOTAL **2 HOURS, 20 MINUTES**

4 cups satsuma orange or
   tangerine juice (from 8 pounds
   oranges or tangerines)

1/2 cup honey

2 tablespoons kosher salt

1 (12-pound) whole fresh or
   frozen turkey, thawed

1/4 cup unsalted butter, softened

1 tablespoon satsuma orange
   zest

2 teaspoons black pepper

2 satsuma oranges, halved

5 rosemary sprigs

5 sage sprigs

4 medium shallots, peeled

2 tablespoons salted butter

3 cups chicken stock

2 tablespoons instant-blending
   flour (such as Wondra)

The holiday bird gets gussied up Southern-style with a shiny glaze of citrus. Use Southern satsumas, a variety of mandarin that grows in the southernmost parts of the Southeast, or Florida citrus.

1 Preheat oven to 400°F. Combine juice, honey, and 1 teaspoon of the salt in a saucepan. Cook over medium-high, stirring occasionally, until reduced to 2 cups and glazy, about 15 to 20 minutes; remove from heat. Reserve ¼ cup orange glaze for gravy. Set remaining orange glaze aside for basting.

2 Remove giblets and neck from turkey, and reserve for another use or discard. Pat turkey dry with paper towels.

3 Combine the unsalted butter, zest, 1 teaspoon of the pepper, and 2 teaspoons of the salt in a small bowl. Starting at the neck, gently loosen and lift skin from turkey with fingers, without totally detaching skin. Rub butter mixture underneath; carefully replace skin. Place satsuma orange halves, rosemary and sage sprigs, and 2 of the shallots in cavity. Tie ends of legs together with heavy string, and tuck wing tips under neck. Place turkey, breast side up, on a lightly greased rack in a lightly greased heavy-bottomed roasting pan. Sprinkle 2 teaspoons of the salt and remaining 1 teaspoon pepper over turkey.

4 Bake, uncovered, in preheated oven for 30 minutes. Rotate roasting pan, and reduce oven temperature to 350°F. Brush about ⅓ cup of the orange glaze over turkey; bake until a meat thermometer inserted into thickest portion of thigh registers 170°F, 1½ to 2 hours, rotating pan and brushing turkey with ⅓ cup orange glaze every 30 minutes. Shield turkey with aluminum foil once turkey is browned to prevent excessive browning, if necessary. Remove turkey to a cutting board; let rest at least 30 minutes.

5 Mince remaining 2 shallots to equal ½ cup. Melt salted butter in a medium skillet over medium-high. Add ½ cup minced shallots, and cook, stirring often, until tender, 2 to 3 minutes. Add stock, remaining 1 teaspoon salt, and reserved ¼ cup orange glaze. Bring to a boil, stirring occasionally; whisk in flour, and cook, stirring often, until slightly thickened, about 5 minutes. Serve with turkey.

Oyster Dressing

SERVES **10** HANDS-ON **25 MINUTES**
TOTAL **1 HOUR, 10 MINUTES**

Some call it "stuffing" but it's doubtful they're from the South because "dressing" is de rigueur below the Mason-Dixon Line. Oyster-and-cornbread dressing is an enduring holiday classic. This recipe gets smoke and porky goodness from bacon and heat from a generous dose of hot sauce. This is kinda a one-pot meal.

- 6 ounces thick-cut bacon slices, chopped (about 6 slices)
- 1 1/2 cups chopped yellow onion (about 1 medium onion)
- 3/4 cup finely chopped carrot (about 2 medium carrots)
- 3/4 cup finely chopped celery (about 3 stalks)
- 6 garlic cloves, minced (about 1 1/2 tablespoons)
- 1 tablespoon chopped fresh thyme
- 5 cups crumbled cornbread (not sweet)
- 1 (9-ounce) package oyster crackers
- 2 cups seafood or chicken stock
- 4 teaspoons hot sauce (such as Crystal)
- 1 1/2 teaspoons kosher salt
- 1 teaspoon black pepper
- 3 large eggs, beaten
- 1 pint shucked oysters, drained
- 1/4 cup melted salted butter

1 Preheat oven to 375°F. Cook bacon in a large skillet over medium-high, stirring occasionally, until crispy, 6 to 8 minutes. Using a slotted spoon, transfer bacon to a plate lined with paper towels, reserving drippings in skillet. Add onion, carrot, celery, garlic, and thyme to reserved drippings in skillet, and cook, stirring occasionally, until onion is translucent and vegetables are slightly softened, 6 to 8 minutes. Remove from the heat, and let cool slightly, about 5 minutes.

2 Combine onion mixture, crumbled cornbread, and crackers in a large bowl. Whisk together stock, hot sauce, salt, pepper, and eggs until smooth. Slowly drizzle into cornbread mixture, tossing gently to moisten. Fold in oysters. Spoon into a lightly greased 13- x 9-inch glass or ceramic baking dish. Sprinkle with cooked bacon, and drizzle with butter. Bake in preheated oven until set and lightly browned, 45 to 50 minutes.

Savory Sorghum-Benne-Sweet Potato Casserole

SERVES **10** HANDS-ON **25 MINUTES**
TOTAL **2 HOURS, 15 MINUTES**

Sweet, but not cloyingly so, this somewhat exotic and perfumy version of the marshmallowy classic is enriched with eggs and butter.

- 3 pounds sweet potatoes (about 6 medium)
- 1/2 cup sorghum syrup
- 4 tablespoons salted butter, melted
- 1 teaspoon vanilla bean paste or extract
- 1 1/2 teaspoons kosher salt
- 1 teaspoon black pepper
- 2 large eggs, separated
- 3/4 cup chopped pecans
- 3/4 cup uncooked old-fashioned regular rolled oats
- 1/3 cup benne (white sesame) seeds
- 2 tablespoons light brown sugar
- 1/2 teaspoon ground cinnamon

1 Preheat oven to 350°F. Wrap potatoes individually in aluminum foil. Place on a rimmed baking sheet, and roast in preheated oven until very tender, 1 hour to 1 hour and 15 minutes. Remove from oven; unwrap and let cool 30 minutes.

2 Scoop sweet potato flesh from skin, discarding skin. Place sweet potatoes in a large bowl; mash until smooth. Stir in sorghum, butter, vanilla, salt, pepper, and egg yolks. Spoon sweet potato mixture into an 8-inch square glass or ceramic baking dish.

3 Place egg whites in a small bowl; whisk until frothy. Stir in pecans, oats, benne seeds, brown sugar, and cinnamon. Sprinkle pecan mixture over sweet potato mixture.

4 Bake in preheated oven until bubbly around edges and lightly browned on top, 40 to 50 minutes.

Blistered Green Beans with Lemony Breadcrumbs

SERVES **10**
HANDS-ON **15 MINUTES**
TOTAL **15 MINUTES**

¼ cup olive oil

2 pounds fresh green beans, trimmed

1 teaspoon kosher salt

½ teaspoon black pepper

¼ cup unsalted butter

2 cups coarse fresh breadcrumbs

1 tablespoon lemon zest (from 2 medium lemons)

2 tablespoons chopped fresh flat-leaf parsley

The slight char on the beans concentrates their flavor while cooking them to a perfect toothsome al dente for a nice change of pace from the expected green bean casserole.

1 Heat 2 tablespoons of the oil in a large skillet over high. Add half of beans, and cook, stirring often, until blistered and tender, about 6 minutes. Season with ½ teaspoon salt and ¼ teaspoon pepper. Transfer to a platter; repeat procedure with remaining oil, beans, salt, and pepper.

2 Melt butter in a nonstick skillet over medium-high until foamy. Add breadcrumbs, and cook, stirring often, until golden and toasted, about 4 minutes. Stir in zest and parsley. Sprinkle breadcrumb mixture evenly over green beans.

Fruitcake Trifle with Bourbon Cream Custard and Spiced Whipped Cream

For this decadent cake (pictured at left), be sure you prepare the Bourbon Cream Custard ahead of time so that it is well chilled.

1 Prepare the Fruitcake: Preheat oven to 300°F. Coat a 13- x 9-inch baking pan with cooking spray. Line bottom with parchment paper; coat paper with cooking spray.

2 Beat butter with a heavy-duty stand mixer on medium speed until creamy, 2 to 3 minutes; add brown sugar and granulated sugar, beating until light and fluffy, 4 to 5 minutes. Beat in molasses; add eggs, 1 at a time, beating well after each addition.

3 Combine buttermilk and baking soda in a 2-cup glass measuring cup (mixture will foam up). Place 3 ½ cups of the flour in a medium bowl. Whisk in cinnamon, allspice, nutmeg, and cloves until blended. Add flour mixture to butter mixture alternately with buttermilk mixture, beginning and ending with flour mixture, beating until combined after each addition. Stir in minced ginger and vanilla. Combine mixed fruits, raisins, golden raisins, and remaining ½ cup flour in a bowl; toss to coat. Fold fruit mixture into batter.

4 Pour batter into prepared baking pan. Bake in preheated oven until a wooden pick inserted in center comes out clean, 50 to 55 minutes. Remove pan to a wire rack, and cool completely, about 1 hour.

5 Prepare the Spiced Whipped Cream: Beat heavy cream and vanilla with an electric mixer on medium-high speed until foamy; gradually add powdered sugar, beating until medium peaks form, 2 to 3 minutes. Chill until ready to use.

6 Cut cake into 2-inch cubes. Using a 4-quart trifle bowl or glass serving bowl, layer one-third of the cake cubes, topped with one-third of the chilled Bourbon Cream Custard, one-third of the Spiced Whipped Cream, and one-third of pecans. Repeat each layer 2 times. Chill at least 4 hours, or overnight before serving.

Bourbon Cream Custard

Whisk together **1 ¼ cups packed brown sugar**, **½ cup cornstarch**, and **½ teaspoon kosher salt** in a large heavy saucepan. Whisk together **5 cups half-and-half** and **8 large egg yolks** in a medium bowl, and slowly pour into saucepan. Cook over medium, whisking constantly, until just starting to bubble, about 10 minutes. Cook, whisking constantly, 1 minute; remove from heat, and add **⅓ cup bourbon** and **6 tablespoons butter**, whisking until butter melts. Transfer mixture to a medium bowl, and place plastic wrap directly onto custard (to prevent a film from forming). Cool 30 minutes. Chill at least 1 hour. SERVES **12 TO 15**

SERVES **12 TO 15**
HANDS-ON **45 MINUTES**
TOTAL **8 HOURS, 30 MINUTES,
INCLUDING CUSTARD AND
4 HOURS CHILLING**

FRUITCAKE
1 cup (8 ounces) salted butter, softened
1 cup packed light brown sugar
½ cup granulated sugar
½ cup dark molasses
2 large eggs
1 cup whole buttermilk
2 teaspoons baking soda
4 cups (about 17 ounces) all-purpose flour
1 teaspoon ground cinnamon
¾ teaspoon ground allspice
½ teaspoon ground nutmeg
¼ teaspoon ground cloves
¼ cup minced crystallized ginger
1 teaspoon vanilla extract
1 ½ cups chopped mixed dried fruits (such as Sun-Maid)
1 cup raisins
1 cup golden raisins

SPICED WHIPPED CREAM
2 cups heavy cream
1 teaspoon vanilla extract
6 tablespoons powdered sugar

ADDITIONAL INGREDIENTS
Bourbon Cream Custard (recipe at left)
2 cups chopped toasted pecans

Chocolate Pecan Pie

This is a nice variation on a classic. Chocolate with a hint of orange from the liqueur puts this firmly in the holiday, special-occasion column. It's ooey-gooey and crispy in all the right places.

1 Prepare the Crust: Melt ¼ tablespoon of the butter in a small skillet over medium, swirling to coat sides of skillet. Add finely chopped pecans, and cook, stirring often, until fragrant and lightly toasted, about 2 minutes. Sprinkle pecan mixture with a pinch of the salt. Remove pecans from skillet, and cool completely, about 20 minutes. Set chopped pecan mixture aside.

2 Pulse flour, sugar, and remaining ½ teaspoon salt in a food processor until well combined, 3 or 4 times. Add cold shortening and remaining cubed cold butter; pulse until mixture resembles coarse meal. Drizzle 3 tablespoons buttermilk over flour mixture, and pulse just until moist clumps form, 10 to 12 pulses. (Add up to 1 additional tablespoon buttermilk, 1 teaspoon at a time, if necessary.) Shape dough into a flat disk, and wrap tightly with plastic wrap. Chill dough at least 1 hour or up to overnight. If chilled longer than 1 hour, let stand at room temperature 10 to 15 minutes before rolling.

3 Meanwhile, prepare the Filling: Bring chocolate chips, corn syrup, sugars, and Southern Comfort to a boil in a large saucepan over medium, whisking constantly. Cook, whisking constantly, 2 minutes; remove from heat. Whisk together eggs, melted butter, cornmeal, vanilla, and salt in a bowl. Gradually whisk about one-fourth of hot corn syrup mixture into egg mixture; gradually add egg mixture to remaining corn syrup mixture, whisking constantly. Stir in pecan halves, and let Filling cool completely, about 30 minutes.

4 Preheat oven to 325°F. Unwrap dough, and roll into a 13-inch circle on a lightly floured surface. Sprinkle dough with chopped pecan mixture. Place a piece of plastic wrap over dough and pecan mixture, and lightly roll pecan mixture into dough. Fit dough into a lightly greased (with cooking spray) 9-inch pie pan. Fold edges under, and crimp. Pour cooled Filling into prepared crust. Bake in preheated oven until set, 1 hour to 1 hour and 5 minutes, shielding edges of crust with aluminum foil after 45 minutes to prevent excessive browning; cool pie completely on a wire rack before slicing, about 3 hours. Serve with sweetened whipped cream or ice cream, if desired.

VARIATION

Mexican Chocolate Pecan Pie

Prepare recipe as directed, adding ⅛ **teaspoon cayenne** and ½ **teaspoon ground cinnamon** to Filling with chocolate in Step 3.

SERVES **10**
HANDS-ON **30 MINUTES**
TOTAL **5 HOURS, 30 MINUTES**

CRUST

4 ½ tablespoons cold cubed salted butter

¼ cup finely chopped pecans

½ teaspoon plus pinch of kosher salt

1 ¼ cups (about 5 ⅜ ounces) all-purpose flour

2 tablespoons granulated sugar

¼ cup cold shortening, cubed

3 to 4 tablespoons buttermilk

FILLING

8 ounces semisweet chocolate chips

1 cup light corn syrup

½ cup granulated sugar

½ cup packed dark brown sugar

¼ cup (2 ounces) Southern Comfort or Grand Marnier

4 large eggs

¼ cup salted butter, melted and cooled

1 tablespoon fine cornmeal

1 teaspoon vanilla extract

¾ teaspoon kosher salt

2 ½ cups lightly toasted pecan halves

ADDITIONAL INGREDIENT

Sweetened whipped cream or vanilla ice cream

RING *in the* NEW...

20

THE HOLIDAYS ARE WINDING DOWN AND THE NEW YEAR IS HERE. KICK THINGS OFF WITH A HEALTHY, VIBRANT BREAKFAST SURE TO PUT PEP IN YOUR STEP ON THAT FAMILY HIKE, DAY ON THE BIKE, OR HOUR SWEATING AT THE GYM. IT'S TIME TO RING IN THE NEW BEGINNINGS.

THE MENU
SERVES 8

Hot Chicory Latte

Iced Tulsi Tea

Spiced Chia Seed
Breakfast Pudding

Grain-Free Breakfast
Bowls

Savory Oatmeal Bowls

Chocolate-Pecan Pie
Protein Bars

Homemade Fruit
Leather

Apple-Pear-Spice
Fruit Leather

Natural Selection

The holiday decor of this home incorporates natural elements at every turn: evergreen and magnolia, thistle and fern, blossom and bud. Cable-knit stockings and wooden accents are cozy counterparts for this relaxed look (left).

Hanging of the Green

Back door or front, no matter where you enter this home you are greeted with pretty accents that bring the outdoors in. A mudroom offers an inviting perch to shed coat and scarf, while one glance at the foyer's towering tree draws visitors inside.

Get the Look

Wooden accents like
wreaths and lathe-
turned trees are
striking decorative
elements that require
little embellishment. A
hardworking galvanized
trolley from the garden
shed becomes a mobile
butler's pantry, keeping
everything the host
needs at arm's reach. A
wintry painting sets the
scene for a collection of
fanciful Christmas trees,
ornaments, and figurine. A
beaded stand, reminiscent
of a colorfully decorated
tree, does double duty as
decorative element on a
rustic sideboard and pretty
serving piece to allow
guests to help themselves.

Hot Chicory Latte

SERVES **8** HANDS-ON **20 MINUTES** TOTAL **20 MINUTES**

This is a practical way to make fancy coffee for a large group. It's simple and you don't need any fancy equipment. The coffee is strong, but the bitterness of chicory is tempered with simple syrup, milk, and nutmeg's distinctive warm flavor.

¼ cup ground chicory coffee beans (such as Café Du Monde)
¼ cup ground dark roast coffee beans
3 cups water

6 cups 2% reduced-fat milk
2 tablespoons plus 2 teaspoons simple syrup
Freshly grated nutmeg

1 Place ground chicory coffee beans and dark roast coffee beans in a coffee filter or filter basket of a drip coffeemaker. Add 3 cups water to coffeemaker, and brew according to manufacturer's instructions.

2 Meanwhile, heat milk in a medium saucepan over medium, stirring occasionally, until milk is thoroughly heated (do not simmer), 8 to 9 minutes.

3 Pour half of hot milk into a large French press; quickly press the plunger up and down until milk at the top is frothy and has the texture of heavy cream, about 1 minute. Pour ½ cup brewed coffee into each of 4 coffee cups. Stir 1 teaspoon simple syrup into each cup. Gently remove plunger from press, and pour ¾ cup milk into each coffee cup, using a spoon to hold back foam while pouring. Spoon foam evenly over lattes.

4 Repeat Step 3 with remaining hot milk, coffee, and syrup. Garnish with nutmeg, and serve immediately.

Iced Tulsi Tea

SERVES **8** HANDS-ON **15 MINUTES** TOTAL **1 HOUR, 25 MINUTES, INCLUDING 1 HOUR CHILLING**

Less astringent than black tea, Tulsi tea is caffeine-free and stress-relieving, so it kills your thirst and your stress!

6 cups water
12 regular-size Tulsi tea bags (such as Organic India Original Tulsi)
⅓ cup granulated sugar (optional)

7 cups ice cubes
1 (3-ounce) lemon, thinly sliced (⅓ cup slices)
Fresh basil leaves

Bring 6 cups water to a boil in a medium saucepan over high. Remove from heat, add tea bags, and steep until water is flavored, 10 minutes. Remove and discard tea bags. Add sugar to tea, if desired, stirring until dissolved. Pour tea into a large pitcher. Stir in ice until melted, about 20 seconds. Add lemon slices, and refrigerate until chilled, about 1 hour. Fill 8 tall (16-ounce) glasses with ice; pour 1 cup tea into each glass. Garnish with basil leaves.

Spiced Chia Seed Breakfast Pudding

SERVES **8** HANDS-ON **25 MINUTES** TOTAL **25 MINUTES, INCLUDING 12 HOURS CHILLING**

If you're a bit dubious of chia seed, particularly in puddings, you must try this. This pudding is only slightly sweet with subtle vanilla flavor and the welcome crunch of pecans. Glazed apples and pears add warmth and richness. This could also stand in for dessert.

2 cups unsweetened vanilla almond milk (such as Almond Breeze)

2 cups plain whole-milk yogurt

¼ cup pure maple syrup

½ teaspoon kosher salt

½ cup (3 ounces) chia seeds

2 tablespoons light brown sugar

¼ teaspoon ground cinnamon

⅛ teaspoon freshly grated nutmeg

⅛ teaspoon ground cardamom

½ teaspoon orange zest, plus 1 teaspoon fresh juice (from 1 orange)

1 tablespoon unsalted butter

1 large (8-ounce) Honeycrisp apple, peeled and cut into ¼-inch-thick slices (about 1 ½ cups)

1 large (8-ounce) Bosc pear, peeled and cut into ¼-inch-thick slices (about 1 cup)

⅔ cup candied pecans, chopped

1 Stir together almond milk, yogurt, maple syrup, and ¼ teaspoon of the salt in a medium bowl until just blended. Whisk in chia seeds; let stand at room temperature 30 minutes, stirring after 15 minutes. Cover and chill 12 hours or overnight.

2 Stir together brown sugar, cinnamon, nutmeg, cardamom, orange zest, and remaining ¼ teaspoon salt in a small bowl; set aside. Melt butter in a medium nonstick skillet over medium-high until foamy. Stir in brown sugar mixture, apple, pear, and orange juice. Cook, stirring occasionally, until apple and pear are tender-crisp and glazed, about 2 minutes. Remove from heat. Spoon ½ cup chia pudding into each of 8 serving bowls; spoon fruit mixture evenly into bowls, and swirl gently. Sprinkle bowls evenly with chopped candied pecans.

Grain-Free Breakfast Bowls

SERVES **8** HANDS-ON **50 MINUTES** TOTAL **50 MINUTES**

This fresh bowl is so loaded with textures you won't miss the grains at all! The egg yolk and pico de gallo are the "sauces" for the bowl, while avocado and egg give richness. Add some grilled chicken, steak, or shrimp for a hearty lunch or dinner bowl.

9 cups water plus 2 tablespoons

8 large eggs

3 tablespoons extra-virgin olive oil

2 medium (9 ounces each) sweet potatoes, spiralized (4 cups)

3 medium (6 ounces each) zucchini, spiralized (4 cups)

2 teaspoons kosher salt

1 large (13-ounce) red onion, thinly sliced (3 cups)

1 (15.5-ounce) can black beans, drained and rinsed (1 ½ cups)

1 cup (5 ounces) pico de gallo (from 1 [1-pound] container)

2 ripe avocados (8 ounces each), cut into ¼-inch-thick slices (2 cups)

4 ounces Cotija cheese, crumbled (about 1 cup)

Fresh cilantro leaves

Lime wedges

1 Bring 9 cups of the water to a boil in a medium saucepan over high. Carefully add eggs, and cook to desired degree of doneness, 6 minutes, 30 seconds for soft-cooked. Remove eggs from water using a slotted spoon, and immediately plunge into a bowl of ice water to stop cooking process; let stand 10 minutes.

2 Meanwhile, heat 1 ½ tablespoons of the oil in a large nonstick skillet over medium-high; swirl to coat. Add spiralized sweet potatoes, and cook, stirring often, until tender-crisp, about 3 minutes. Add zucchini and remaining 2 tablespoons water; cook, stirring often, until tender, about 3 minutes. Transfer sweet potato mixture to a large bowl, and toss with ½ teaspoon of the salt. Wipe skillet clean. Heat remaining 1 ½ tablespoons oil in skillet over medium-high. Add onion, and cook, without stirring, until slightly browned on 1 side, about 4 minutes. Stir onion, and cook, stirring often, until softened, 3 to 4 minutes. Remove from heat; transfer to bowl with sweet potato mixture. Stir in black beans and remaining 1 ½ teaspoons salt until thoroughly blended.

3 Remove eggs from water; crack, peel, and halve eggs. Spoon about ⅔ cup sweet potato mixture into each of 8 bowls. Top evenly with pico de gallo, avocado slices, Cotija cheese, and egg halves. Garnish with cilantro leaves and a lime wedge.

Savory Oatmeal Bowls

These are the very same ingredients that make up a Denver omelet only served in oatmeal for a very substantial start to your day.

1 Heat 1 ½ tablespoons of the olive oil in a large skillet over high. Add ham; cook, stirring often, until crispy and slightly browned, about 4 minutes. Transfer ham to a large plate, reserving drippings in skillet. Add 1 ½ tablespoons of the oil to reserved drippings in skillet, and heat over medium-high. Add onion, and cook, stirring occasionally, until softened and slightly browned, 6 to 7 minutes. Transfer onion to a large bowl, reserving drippings in skillet; toss onion with ½ teaspoon of the salt, and set aside. Add remaining 1 ½ tablespoons oil to reserved drippings in skillet; heat over medium-high. Add red and green bell peppers, and cook, stirring often, until softened, about 8 minutes. Add garlic and thyme; cook, stirring often, until fragrant, about 1 minute. Remove from heat; stir in vinegar. Transfer to bowl with onions; stir in 1 teaspoon hot sauce and ¼ teaspoon of the salt.

2 Bring chicken broth, thyme sprigs, 4 cups of the water, and remaining 1 teaspoon salt to a boil in a large saucepan over high. Stir in oats; reduce heat to low, and simmer, stirring occasionally, until oats are tender, 10 to 12 minutes.

3 Meanwhile, melt 1 tablespoon of the butter in a large skillet with lid over medium-high until foamy. Carefully crack 4 eggs, 1 at a time, into skillet. Cook, undisturbed, until whites are slightly set but yolks are still runny, about 1 minute. Sprinkle 2 tablespoons cheese over each egg, and add 1 tablespoon of the water to skillet; cover with lid, and cook until whites are set, yolks are runny, and cheese is melted, about 1 minute. Transfer to a large plate. Repeat procedure with remaining butter, eggs, cheese, and water.

4 Divide oatmeal among 8 bowls. Spoon onion mixture evenly over oatmeal. Top each bowl with 1 egg and 1 ½ tablespoons ham. Sprinkle eggs with salt to taste, and garnish with a dash of hot sauce.

SERVES **8**
HANDS-ON **50 MINUTES**
TOTAL **50 MINUTES**

---

4 ½ tablespoons olive oil

3 country ham biscuit-cut (or center-cut) slices (6 ounces), halved crosswise and cut into strips (1 cup strips) from 1 (8-ounce) package

1 large (12-ounce) red onion, thinly sliced (2 cups sliced)

1 ¾ teaspoons kosher salt, plus more for serving

1 large (9-ounce) red bell pepper, thinly sliced (1 ¾ cups)

1 large (7-ounce) green bell pepper, thinly sliced (1 ⅓ cups)

1 tablespoon minced garlic (about 3 cloves)

1 teaspoon thyme leaves

1 tablespoon red wine vinegar

1 teaspoon hot sauce (such as Crystal), plus more for garnish

3 cups lower-sodium chicken broth

4 thyme sprigs

4 cups plus 2 tablespoons water

4 cups uncooked old-fashioned regular rolled oats (such as Quaker Oats)

2 tablespoons unsalted butter

8 large eggs

4 ounces extra-sharp Cheddar cheese, shredded (about 1 cup)

Chocolate-Pecan Pie Protein Bars

SERVES 12
HANDS-ON 20 MINUTES
TOTAL 1 HOUR, 20 MINUTES

---

2 ½ cups pecan halves (about 9 ounces)

1 cup coarsely chopped pitted Medjool dates (6 ounces)

¾ cup unflavored egg white protein powder (such as Jay Robb) (2 ½ ounces)

1 teaspoon light brown sugar

¼ teaspoon plus ⅛ teaspoon ground cinnamon

¼ teaspoon kosher salt

2 tablespoons pure maple syrup

3 tablespoons water

½ cup (4 ounces) miniature semisweet chocolate chips

Packed with energy and protein, these homemade bars are perfectly portable and a delicious way to refuel on the go.

1 Pulse pecans, dates, protein powder, brown sugar, cinnamon, and salt in a food processor until finely crumbled, about 6 pulses. With processor running, pour maple syrup and water through food chute, and process until mixture just comes together, about 10 seconds. Transfer mixture to a medium bowl; knead in chocolate chips.

2 Shape mixture into a rectangle, and flatten between 2 sheets of parchment paper. Using a rolling pin, roll mixture into a 10- x 8-inch rectangle (½ inch thick). Chill at least 1 hour or up to overnight. Cut into 12 bars. Wrap each protein bar individually in plastic wrap, and store in refrigerator up to 1 week.

Homemade Fruit Leather

MAKES **20 FRUIT LEATHER STRIPS**
HANDS-ON **35 MINUTES** TOTAL **3 HOURS, 45 MINUTES**

You won't miss all the added sugar or artificial taste of store-bought fruit leather after one taste of these. They have a nice sour tang and chewiness.

- 4 cups fresh raspberries (18 ounces)
- 4 cups fresh blueberries (18 ounces)
- 1 cup pomegranate arils (6 ounces)
- 1 teaspoon lemon zest, plus 2 to 3 teaspoons fresh juice
- 1 cup water
- 2 to 3 tablespoons granulated sugar

1 Combine raspberries, blueberries, pomegranate arils, zest, and water in a medium saucepan. Bring to a simmer over medium, stirring occasionally; cover and cook until berries have burst, 5 minutes. Uncover and stir in desired amount of sugar and lemon juice. Reduce heat to low, and cook, uncovered, stirring occasionally, until mixture has thickened, about 10 minutes.

2 Puree fruit mixture in a high-powered blender until smooth, about 20 seconds. Pour through a fine wire-mesh strainer into a large measuring cup.

3 Lightly coat a half sheet pan or rimmed baking sheet with cooking spray; line with plastic wrap. Pour fruit puree onto plastic wrap, and using a small offset spatula, spread into an even ⅛-inch-thick layer. Tap baking sheet on counter several times to level the mixture. Place baking sheet in a cold oven, and heat to 170°F. Bake until leather is no longer sticky and surface is smooth, 3 hours and 10 minutes to 3 hours and 30 minutes. Let stand at room temperature until slightly cool, about 10 minutes. Invert fruit leather onto a cutting board, and peel off plastic wrap. Cut into 20 (1-inch-wide) strips. Roll each strip, and wrap in plastic wrap; place in an airtight container. Store at room temperature up to 1 week, refrigerate up to 1 month, or freeze up to 3 months.

Apple-Pear-Spice Fruit Leather

MAKES **10 FRUIT LEATHER STRIPS**
HANDS-ON **25 MINUTES** TOTAL **5 HOURS, 45 MINUTES**

These fruit leathers do take a long time to make, but it's a set-it-and-forget-it situation so it's mostly hands-off time.

- 3 cups peeled and thinly sliced Honeycrisp apples (from 2 medium [10 ounces each] apples)
- 3 cups peeled and thinly sliced Bosc pears (from 4 medium [5 ounces each] pears)
- ½ cup water
- ½ teaspoon fresh lemon juice (from 1 lemon)
- ½ teaspoon ground cinnamon
- 1 to 2 tablespoons granulated sugar

1 Combine apples, pears, and ¼ cup water in a medium saucepan. Cook, covered, over medium, stirring occasionally, until slightly softened, 10 minutes. Remove from heat, uncover, and coarsely mash fruit mixture with a potato masher. Add lemon juice, cinnamon, and desired amount of sugar. Cook, uncovered, over medium, stirring occasionally, until mixture has thickened and most of the water has evaporated, 20 to 25 minutes.

2 Transfer fruit mixture to a high-powered blender. Remove center piece of blender lid (to allow steam to escape); secure lid on blender, and place a clean towel over opening in lid (to prevent splatters). Puree until smooth, about 20 seconds.

3 Lightly coat a half sheet pan or rimmed baking sheet with cooking spray; line with plastic wrap. Pour fruit puree onto plastic wrap, and using a small offset spatula, spread mixture into an even ⅛-inch-thick layer. Tap baking sheet on counter several times to level the mixture. Place baking sheet in a cold oven, and heat to 170°F. Bake until leather is no longer sticky and surface is smooth, 4 hours and 45 minutes to 5 hours. Invert fruit leather onto a cutting board, and peel off plastic wrap. Cut into 10 (1-inch-wide) strips. Roll each strip, and wrap in plastic wrap; place in an airtight container. Store at room temperature up to 1 week, refrigerate up to 1 month, or freeze up to 3 months.

Savor

SOUP'S ON

BABY IT'S COLD OUTSIDE . . . SO RELAX BY THE FIRE WITH
FRIENDS AND FAMILY WHILE ONE OF THESE SOUL-WARMING
POTS OF GOODNESS SIMMERS ON THE STOVETOP.

Chicken Noodle Soup with Poached Egg

SERVES **10** HANDS-ON **1 HOUR**
TOTAL **3 HOURS, 50 MINUTES**

This classic cures-what-ails-you bowl is enriched with the sunny yolk of a poached egg, which lends richness to the broth.

CHICKEN STOCK
3 ½ pounds chicken wings
4 quarts water
2 (10-ounce) yellow onions, quartered
2 large carrots, coarsely chopped (9 ounces chopped)
3 celery stalks, coarsely chopped (5 ounces chopped)
8 garlic cloves, smashed
7 whole allspice
8 thyme sprigs
10 flat-leaf parsley sprigs
2 bay leaves
1 ½ teaspoons black peppercorns

SOUP
3 tablespoons olive oil
1 (10-ounce) large onion, chopped (2 cups)
5 celery stalks, cut into small cubes (2 cups)

3 medium carrots, cut into ½-inch-thick slices (about 1 ½ cups)
3 garlic cloves, minced (about 1 tablespoon)
1 tablespoon kosher salt
1 teaspoon chopped fresh thyme
1 teaspoon dried marjoram
1 teaspoon black pepper
8 ounces uncooked extra-wide egg noodles
4 cups shredded rotisserie chicken (about 1 pound)
2 tablespoons fresh lemon juice (from 1 lemon)
8 large eggs
4 teaspoons chopped fresh chives

1 Prepare the Chicken Stock: Bring all ingredients to a boil in a large stockpot over high. Reduce heat to low; cover and simmer, skimming and discarding foam as needed, 2 ½ to 3 hours. Remove large solids from stock, and discard. Pour stock through a fine wire-mesh strainer or a colander lined with cheesecloth into a large bowl, discarding solids. Set 3 quarts of Chicken Stock aside; reserve remaining stock for another use.

2 Prepare the Soup: Heat oil in a Dutch oven over medium-high. Add onion, celery, carrots, and garlic; cook, stirring occasionally, until softened, about 10 minutes. Stir in salt, thyme, marjoram, and pepper; cook, stirring often, until spices are fragrant, about 3 minutes. Stir in 3 quarts prepared Chicken Stock; bring to a boil. Stir in noodles, and cook until almost tender, about 8 minutes. Stir in shredded chicken and 1 tablespoon of the lemon juice. Cook until chicken is warmed through, about 2 minutes. Reduce heat to low, and keep warm until ready to use.

3 Pour water to a depth of 2 inches into a large saucepan, and stir in remaining 1 tablespoon lemon juice. Bring to a boil over high; reduce heat to low. Break 4 eggs, 1 at a time, into a ramekin, and slip each egg into water, as close to surface as possible. Cook, undisturbed, until whites are opaque and yolks are runny, about 3 minutes. Using a slotted spoon, transfer eggs, 1 at a time, from pan to a plate lined with paper towels. Repeat procedure with remaining eggs.

4 Ladle soup into 8 bowls; place 1 egg in center of each. Sprinkle with chives, and serve.

Pasta Shape Primer

There are no firm rules for matching a pasta shape to a sauce, but there are some general tips to make the matching game easier:

LONG SHAPES
Spaghetti, fettuccine, linguine, vermicelli, and angel hair are the most popular and versatile. Team thick strands with hearty sauces and thin strands with light, delicate sauces.

MEDIUM SHAPES
Penne, rigatoni, and mostaccioli have holes and ridges that pair well with chunkier sauces. Farfalle (bow ties), elbow macaroni, radiatori (little radiators), wagon wheels, and shells are popular in pasta salads, baked casseroles, and hearty stews.

SMALL SHAPES
Ditalini (thimbles) and orzo (rice-shaped) are suited for soups, salads, or mixed with sauces as a side dish starch.

EGG NOODLES
Available in fine, medium, and wide, these are commonly used in casseroles, soups, and as a base for stews. As the name implies, egg noodles contain egg, while not all pastas do.

SPECIALTY SHAPES
Lasagna, manicotti, and jumbo shells are always used in baked dishes. Ravioli and tortellini are filled with meat, cheese, or other ingredients.

Creamy Pumpkin Soup

SERVES **10** HANDS-ON **30 MINUTES** TOTAL **1 HOUR**

All the spices you might expect in pumpkin pie find their way into this savory soup that gets a sweet note from Honeycrisp apples.

1 whole star anise	1 ¾ cups chopped
1 cinnamon stick	Honeycrisp apple
¼ teaspoon whole	(from 2 apples)
allspice	2 (15-ounce) cans
1 teaspoon black	pumpkin
peppercorns	5 cups vegetable broth
2 bay leaves	1 ¼ teaspoons kosher
5 thyme sprigs	salt
9 tablespoons	1 cup raw pumpkin seed
(4 ½ ounces) unsalted	kernels (pepitas)
butter, cut into pieces	¼ teaspoon cayenne
1 cup chopped yellow	pepper
onion (from 1 medium	½ teaspoon granulated
onion)	sugar
	1 cup heavy cream

1 Place a 5-inch square of cheesecloth on a flat surface. Add the first 6 ingredients to the center of the square. Gather the edges together; tie securely with kitchen twine. Set the spice bundle aside.

2 Melt 8 tablespoons of the butter in a Dutch oven over medium until foamy, 2 to 3 minutes. Cook, stirring constantly to loosen brown bits from the bottom of the skillet, until butter is golden brown with a nutty aroma, 5 to 7 minutes. Stir in onion and apple; cook, stirring often, until softened, 6 minutes. Add pumpkin, broth, and 1 teaspoon of the salt; stir to combine. Add the spice bundle. Bring the pumpkin mixture to a boil over medium-high; reduce heat to low. Simmer, uncovered, 25 to 30 minutes.

3 Meanwhile, cook remaining 1 tablespoon butter in a medium skillet over medium-high until foamy, 2 to 3 minutes. Add pumpkin seed kernels, and cook, stirring occasionally, 3 minutes. Sprinkle with cayenne, sugar, and remaining ¼ teaspoon salt; cook, stirring, until kernels are toasted, about 3 minutes. Transfer to a paper towel-lined plate; set aside.

4 Remove the spice bundle from the pumpkin mixture, and discard. Transfer half of mixture to a blender. Remove center of blender lid (to allow steam to escape); secure lid on blender, and place a clean towel over opening in lid (to prevent splatters). Process until smooth, about 30 seconds. Transfer to a large bowl. Repeat process with remaining mixture. Return pumpkin to Dutch oven; stir in heavy cream.

5 Divide soup evenly among 10 soup bowls. Sprinkle with pumpkin seed kernels.

Smoky Lentil Soup

SERVES **8** HANDS-ON **1 HOUR, 35 MINUTES** TOTAL **1 HOUR, 35 MINUTES**

Bacon and Spanish smoked paprika lend a wisp of smokehouse flavor to this hearty classic, while a splash of sherry vinegar adds brightness to every spoonful.

2 tablespoons olive oil	1 tablespoon smoked
1 (12-ounce) package	paprika
center-cut bacon,	2 teaspoons ground
cut into 1-inch pieces	cumin
(about 14 slices)	2 tablespoons chopped
2 cups chopped yellow	fresh thyme
onion (from 1 medium	2 cups dried brown lentils
yellow onion)	(16 ounces)
1 cup chopped carrot	2 teaspoons kosher salt
(from 3 medium	6 cups vegetable broth
carrots)	3 cups crushed tomatoes
3 tablespoons minced	(from 1 [28-ounce]
garlic (from 9 garlic	can)
cloves)	1 large (6-ounce)
2 tablespoons tomato	bunch lacinato kale,
paste	stemmed and thinly
	sliced (about 4 cups)
	1 tablespoon sherry
	vinegar

1 Heat oil in a Dutch oven over medium. Add bacon, cook, stirring occasionally, until lightly browned but still tender, 8 to 10 minutes. Stir in onion, carrot, and garlic, and cook, stirring occasionally, until softened, 3 to 4 minutes. Stir in tomato paste, paprika, cumin, thyme, lentils, and salt; cook, stirring often, until tomato paste darkens and spices are fragrant, 3 to 4 minutes. Stir in broth, and bring to a boil over high. Reduce heat to low, and simmer, uncovered, stirring occasionally, until lentils are tender, about 1 hour; stir in tomatoes. Remove from heat.

2 Transfer half of lentil mixture to a blender. Remove center piece of blender lid (to allow steam to escape); secure blender lid on blender, and place a clean towel over opening in lid (to prevent splatters). Process until smooth, about 2 to 3 minutes. Return pureed lentil mixture to Dutch oven, and stir to combine.

3 Bring lentil mixture to a simmer over medium-high. Stir in kale; cook, stirring occasionally, until wilted, 2 to 3 minutes. Remove from heat; stir in sherry vinegar. Divide the soup evenly among 8 bowls.

Shepherd's Pie Soup

SERVES **12** HANDS-ON **45 MINUTES** TOTAL **2 HOURS**

This soup riff on the old English savory pie is meat-and-potatoes at their savory best.

SOUP
2 tablespoons olive oil
2 cups chopped onion
4 carrots, cut into small cubes (2 ¾ cups)
2 tablespoons minced garlic (about 6 cloves)
1 tablespoon chopped fresh thyme
1 ½ pounds ground lamb
1 teaspoon kosher salt
½ teaspoon black pepper
¼ cup dry white wine
3 tablespoons all-purpose flour
3 tablespoons tomato paste
1 tablespoon Worcestershire sauce
11 cups beef broth

3 cups frozen peas, thawed
2 cups frozen pearl onions, thawed
1 (15-ounce) can corn kernels, drained

MASHED POTATOES
2 pounds russet potatoes, cubed
1 tablespoon plus ¾ teaspoon kosher salt
6 cups cold water
⅓ cup heavy cream
8 tablespoons (4 ounces) unsalted butter, cut into pieces
2 large egg yolks
¼ teaspoon black pepper, plus more for garnish

1. Heat oil in a Dutch oven over medium-high. Add the onion and carrots; sauté 7 minutes. Add garlic and thyme; sauté 1 minute. Add the lamb, salt, and pepper. Sauté until meat is browned, 13 minutes.

2. Add the wine, stirring to deglaze. Stir in flour; cook 1 minute. Whisk in tomato paste, Worcestershire sauce, and broth. Bring to a boil; reduce to a simmer. Cook until thickened and flavors meld, about 20 minutes. Skim fat from surface. Stir in peas, pearl onions, and corn. Cook 2 minutes more.

3. Preheat the oven to 425°F. Bring the potatoes, 1 tablespoon salt, and 6 cups water to a boil in a saucepan over high. Reduce heat. Simmer, uncovered, until fork-tender, 12 minutes; drain. Cool 5 minutes. Press through a food mill or ricer into the saucepan.

4. Heat cream and 6 tablespoons butter in a small saucepan over medium, stirring, until melted (do not boil), about 3 minutes. Stir mixture into the potatoes. Add egg yolks, ¼ teaspoon pepper and remaining ¾ teaspoon salt; stir to combine.

5. Spoon potatoes into 3-inch mounds on a parchment-lined baking sheet. Melt remaining butter. Brush mounds; garnish with pepper. Bake until golden, 20 to 25 minutes.

6. Divide soup among 12 bowls. Place a potato puff in the center of each bowl. Serve immediately.

French Onion Soup

SERVES **10** HANDS-ON **1 HOUR** TOTAL **2 HOURS**

Hearty broth, sweet onion, and aged cheeses offer a burst of umami in every bite.

3 pounds chicken wings (15 to 16 wings)
12 cups chicken broth
5 tablespoons (2 ½ ounces) unsalted butter, cut into pieces
5 pounds yellow onions, thinly sliced (about 6 large onions)
1 ½ teaspoons kosher salt
3 thyme sprigs, plus more for garnish
1 teaspoon black peppercorns

1 bay leaf
3 flat-leaf parsley sprigs
½ cup dry sherry
10 ounces Asiago cheese, grated (about 2 ½ cups)
10 ounces Gruyère cheese, shredded (about 2 ½ cups)
10 (½-inch-thick) baguette slices, toasted
1 large garlic clove, halved

1. Combine wings and chicken broth in a large stockpot. Boil over high; reduce to medium, and simmer about 40 minutes. Pour through a fine wire-mesh strainer into a large bowl. Set aside.

2. Heat butter in a large Dutch oven over medium until foamy, about 3 minutes. Stir in onions and 1 teaspoon of the salt. Partially cover, reduce heat to medium-low, and cook, stirring, until softened, 20 minutes. Uncover and cook, stirring often, until golden brown, about 1 hour and 15 minutes.

3. Meanwhile, place a 5-inch square of cheesecloth on a flat surface. Arrange thyme, peppercorns, bay leaf, and parsley in center of square. Gather edges together; tie with kitchen twine. Set aside.

4. Stir sherry into onions, stirring to deglaze. Stir in prepared chicken stock. Add herb bundle. Bring to a boil over high; reduce to medium-low. Simmer, stirring, until flavors meld, about 10 minutes. Stir in remaining salt.

5. Preheat broiler to high with oven rack 6 inches from heat. Stir together Asiago and Gruyère cheeses in a medium bowl; set aside.

6. Rub toasted baguette slices with cut sides of garlic. Remove and discard herb bundle from soup. Ladle about 1 ¼ cups soup into 10 broiler-safe soup bowls arranged on 2 rimmed baking sheets. Sprinkle ¼ cup cheese mixture over each bowl. Place a baguette slice in the center of each bowl, and sprinkle each with ¼ cup cheese mixture. Place 1 baking sheet in oven, and broil until cheese is melted and golden brown, about 2 minutes. Repeat with remaining baking sheet. Garnish each with thyme sprigs, if desired, and serve.

Beef Consommé with Winter Vegetables

SERVES **10 TO 12** HANDS-ON **2 HOURS**
TOTAL **14 HOURS, 45 MINUTES, INCLUDING
8 HOURS CHILLING**

Consommé is a clarified meat broth served hot or chilled as a soup, or used as a base for sauces.

BEEF STOCK
5 pounds beef bones
2 pounds chicken wings
2 pounds beef stew meat
2 cups dry red wine
3 pounds yellow onions, halved
1 ½ pounds celery stalks, cut into thirds
1 ½ pounds carrots, cut into thirds
5 quarts water
¼ cup tomato paste
5 thyme sprigs
2 rosemary sprigs
7 flat-leaf parsley sprigs
1 garlic head, cut in half crosswise
1 tablespoon black peppercorns
1 tablespoon kosher salt

CLARIFICATION RAFT
4 large egg whites
1 pound ⁹⁰/₁₀ lean ground sirloin
2 cups chopped tomato
5 flat-leaf parsley sprigs
1 large yellow onion, thinly sliced
1 large carrot, shaved into ribbons

WINTER VEGETABLES
1 (1 ¼-pound) butternut squash, peeled and diced
2 large parsnips, peeled and diced
1 large leek, white part only, diced
1 large sweet potato, peeled and diced

HERBED CROUTONS
3 garlic cloves, thinly sliced
3 thyme sprigs
½ rosemary sprig
¾ cup olive oil
1 (1-pound) rustic Italian bread loaf, cubed
½ teaspoon kosher salt
½ teaspoon black pepper

1 Prepare the Beef Stock: Preheat oven to 400°F. Place racks in upper and lower thirds of oven. Arrange bones and wings in a single layer on a rimmed baking sheet. Arrange beef stew meat in a single layer on a second rimmed baking sheet. Place baking sheets on separate racks; bake until deeply browned, 45 minutes to 1 hour, rotating and switching pans halfway through. Remove from oven. Transfer ingredients from baking sheets to a 12-quart stockpot; add ½ cup wine to each baking sheet, scraping to loosen browned bits from pan bottoms. Pour liquid from pans into the stockpot.

2 Arrange onions, celery, and carrots on 2 rimmed baking sheets, and roast at 400°F until browned, 35 minutes, rotating and switching pans halfway

through. Remove and transfer vegetables to stockpot with bone mixture. Add ½ cup wine to each baking sheet, scraping to loosen browned bits from pan bottoms. Pour liquid from pans into the stockpot.

3 Add water, tomato paste, thyme, rosemary, parsley, garlic, and peppercorns to stockpot; stir once. Boil over high. Reduce to medium; simmer gently to concentrate flavors, 3 to 4 hours. Skim fat and foam from surface. Stir in salt. Pour through a fine wire-mesh strainer into a large pot, and refrigerate 8 hours or up to overnight.

4 Prepare the Clarification Raft: Whisk egg whites in a bowl until frothy, 30 seconds. Add ground sirloin, tomato, parsley, onion, and carrot. Mix with hands to combine. Stir into chilled Beef Stock.

5 Simmer over medium, stirring, to keep meat from sticking to pot. Do not boil. Egg white mixture will rise and form a raft on the surface. Move the pot slightly off the heat to create a convection. (Broth will simmer on 1 side of the pot.) Break a hole in the raft on the simmering side to allow a small ladle to fit through. Continue to simmer over medium, occasionally ladling stock over raft (to prevent it from drying out), until desired clarity is reached, about 1 hour. (Check clarity by ladling broth into a bowl.) Remove broth from heat and ladle through a fine wire-mesh strainer lined with a double layer of cheesecloth into a separate large pot. Be careful to keep the raft intact as you ladle. Discard raft and solids. Skim and discard any fat from surface of consommé. Keep warm over low.

6 Prepare the Winter Vegetables: Bring a stockpot of salted water to a boil. Add squash; cook until softened, about 1 minute. Transfer the squash with a slotted spoon to ice water to shock. Transfer to a paper towel-lined plate. Repeat process with parsnips, leek, and sweet potato, cooking each separately. Set vegetables and salted hot water aside.

7 Prepare the Herbed Croutons: Preheat the oven to 350°F. Bring garlic, thyme, rosemary, and oil to a simmer over low. Cook, stirring, until fragrant and herbs are dark, 10 minutes. Remove. Cool 10 minutes. Press oil mixture through a wire-mesh strainer with a spatula into a bowl. Discard solids.

8 Toss bread cubes with oil, salt, and pepper, and layer on a rimmed baking sheet. Bake until golden brown, about 20 minutes, stirring halfway through.

9 Bring a pot of salted water to a boil over high. Add cooked squash, parsnips, leek, and sweet potato. Cook until warmed through, about 20 seconds. Transfer vegetables with a strainer from water to a paper towel-lined plate. Divide among 10 to 12 bowls. Ladle consommé over vegetables. Top with croutons.

Southern Wedding Soup

SERVES **10** HANDS-ON **50 MINUTES**
TOTAL **1 HOUR, 20 MINUTES**

Wedding soup, the Italian "minestra maritata," refers to the marriage of the greens and meat in the soup. Here, spicy Louisiana andouille and collards drive home Southern flavors.

MEATBALLS
12 ounces raw andouille sausage, diced
1 ¼ pounds ground pork
½ cup finely chopped, stemmed fresh collard greens (about 1 ounce)
3 garlic cloves, smashed
1 cup finely chopped yellow onion
1 ½ ounces Asiago cheese, grated
⅓ cup ricotta cheese
2 tablespoons extra-virgin olive oil
1 large egg, beaten
1 cup dry breadcrumbs
½ teaspoon kosher salt

SOUP
2 tablespoons olive oil
1 ½ cups finely chopped yellow onion
1 tablespoon minced garlic (from 3 cloves)
½ cup dry white wine
12 cups chicken stock
8 ounces uncooked pipette pasta
6 cups coarsely chopped, stemmed collards
1 (15-ounce) can black-eyed peas, drained and rinsed
1 tablespoon kosher salt
1 ½ tablespoons fresh lemon juice
3 ounces Asiago cheese, grated

1 Prepare the Meatballs: Preheat oven to 400°F with oven rack 6 inches from heat.

2 Process andouille in a food processor until finely crumbled, about 20 seconds. Add pork, collard greens, garlic, and onion to food processor; pulse until combined, 5 to 6 times. Transfer mixture to a large bowl, and stir in Asiago cheese, ricotta cheese, olive oil, egg, breadcrumbs, and salt, stirring gently to combine. Shape mixture into 54 (1 ½-inch) meatballs, and place on 2 parchment paper-lined rimmed baking sheets. Bake in preheated oven for 10 minutes. Without removing baking sheets from oven, increase temperature to broil, and broil until browned, 4 to 5 minutes, stirring after 2 minutes.

3 Prepare the Soup: Heat oil in a large Dutch oven over medium-high. Add onion and garlic; cook, stirring occasionally, until softened, about 5 minutes. Stir in wine, and cook until slightly reduced, about 3 minutes. Stir in chicken stock, and bring to a boil over high. Add pasta, and cook until al dente, about 8 minutes. Reduce heat to medium; stir in collards and black-eyed peas; cook until greens are just wilted and peas are heated through, about 3 minutes. Stir in salt and lemon juice. Ladle soup into 10 bowls, and sprinkle each with 2 tablespoons Asiago cheese.

Wild Mushroom Soup

SERVES **12** HANDS-ON **45 MINUTES**
TOTAL **1 HOUR, 30 MINUTES**

This soup is packed with earthy flavor thanks to a medley of mushrooms. Clean fresh mushrooms with a brush or paper towel. If rinsed, they absorb too much moisture and lose texture and flavor.

10 cups vegetable broth
8 cups dried shiitake mushrooms (4 ounces)
6 tablespoons (3 ounces) unsalted butter, cut into pieces
2 cups chopped yellow onion (from 1 onion)
10 ½ cups assorted fresh wild mushrooms, sliced (1 pound, 9 ounces)
7 garlic cloves, chopped
1 tablespoon chopped fresh thyme, plus more for garnish
½ teaspoon freshly ground pepper
1 teaspoon kosher salt
½ cup (4 ounces) brandy
1 cup heavy cream
¼ cup chopped fresh chives

1 Bring broth and dried mushrooms to a boil in a large saucepan over high. Remove from heat, and let stand at room temperature until mushrooms soften, about 30 minutes.

2 Meanwhile, melt butter in a Dutch oven over medium-high, without stirring, until butter begins to foam, 2 to 3 minutes. Continue to cook, stirring constantly with a wooden spoon to loosen brown particles from bottom of Dutch oven, until butter is golden brown and has a nutty aroma, 4 to 6 minutes. Stir in onion and fresh mushrooms; cook, stirring occasionally, until softened and lightly browned, 10 to 12 minutes. Remove and reserve 1 cup browned mushrooms for serving. Stir garlic, thyme, pepper, and salt into mushroom mixture; cook, stirring often, until fragrant, about 1 minute. Add brandy; cook, stirring constantly, until liquid evaporates, 2 to 3 minutes. Stir in softened dried mushrooms and vegetable broth. Bring to a boil over high; reduce heat to low, and simmer, stirring occasionally, until thickened, 15 to 20 minutes.

3 Transfer half of mushroom mixture to a blender. Remove center piece of blender lid (to allow steam to escape); secure blender lid on blender, and place a clean towel over opening in lid (to prevent splatters). Process until very smooth, about 1 to 2 minutes. Transfer to a large bowl. Repeat procedure with remaining mushroom mixture. Return mushroom mixture to Dutch oven, and stir in heavy cream. Cook over high, stirring occasionally, until hot, about 2 minutes.

4 Divide soup evenly among 12 soup bowls. Sprinkle with chopped chives, and garnish with chopped fresh thyme and 1 cup reserved browned mushrooms.

Oyster Chowder

SERVES **12** HANDS-ON **30 MINUTES** TOTAL **55 MINUTES**

Thick, hearty chowders are traditionally made from fish or shellfish with potatoes and other vegetables. Manhattan-style chowders have a tomato base. This recipe is prepared in the New England style because it is enriched with cream.

12 center-cut bacon slices, cut into ½-inch pieces
1 (14-ounce) white onion, finely chopped
1 cup finely chopped celery (from 4 stalks)
1 tablespoon chopped fresh thyme
Pinch of cayenne pepper
2 bay leaves
2 tablespoons all-purpose flour
4 cups half-and-half
4 cups heavy cream
2 teaspoons Worcestershire sauce
2 pounds russet potatoes, cut into ½-inch cubes (about 2 large potatoes)
2 teaspoons kosher salt
6 cups fresh shucked oysters with any oyster liquor (about 120 oysters with oyster liquor)
1 ½ cups oyster crackers (such as Westminster Bakers Co.)

1 Cook bacon in a Dutch oven over medium, stirring occasionally, until crisp, about 8 minutes. Stir in onion, celery, thyme, cayenne, and bay leaves; cook, stirring occasionally, until softened, 3 to 4 minutes. Add flour, and cook, stirring constantly, until thoroughly combined with bacon and vegetable mixture, about 1 minute.

2 Stir in half-and-half, cream, Worcestershire sauce, potatoes, and salt. Bring to a simmer, and cook, stirring occasionally, until potatoes are tender, about 25 to 30 minutes. Add oysters and any oyster liquor, and simmer, stirring occasionally until oysters begin to curl, about 10 minutes.

3 Remove chowder from heat, and discard bay leaves. Divide chowder evenly among 12 bowls, and sprinkle evenly with oyster crackers.

Christmas Gumbo

SERVES **10**
HANDS-ON **40 MINUTES**
TOTAL **2 HOURS, 20 MINUTES**

SHELLFISH STOCK

¼ cup canola oil

1 pound shrimp shells

1 (12-ounce) yellow onion, peeled and quartered

2 celery stalks, coarsely chopped (about 1 ½ cups)

5 bay leaves

5 thyme sprigs

8 garlic cloves, smashed

1 tablespoon black peppercorns

3 quarts water

GUMBO

1 ½ cups canola oil

2 ⅓ cups (about 10 ounces) all-purpose flour

1 (6-ounce) yellow onion, chopped (about 2 cups)

3 celery stalks, cut into ¼-inch cubes (about 1 cup)

2 green bell peppers, chopped (about 2 cups)

1 tablespoon minced garlic (from 3 medium garlic cloves)

2 ½ tablespoons Creole seasoning (such as Tony Chachere's)

1 tablespoon filé powder

2 teaspoons hot sauce

3 bay leaves

½ teaspoon kosher salt

1 pound large peeled, deveined raw shrimp, tail-on

1 pint fresh shucked oysters, drained

1 (1-pound) can lump crabmeat, drained and picked over

Hot cooked long-grain white rice

Thinly sliced scallions

When a roux is cooked to the dark stage, as is done in most gumbo recipes, it loses much of its thickening power; that's why you'll often find filé powder added after the gumbo has cooked. It is a thickener made from dried, ground sassafras leaves.

1 Prepare the Shellfish Stock: Heat oil in a large stainless steel Dutch oven over medium-high. Add shrimp shells, and cook, stirring occasionally, until orange, about 4 minutes. Stir in onion, celery, bay leaves, thyme, garlic, peppercorns, and water. Bring to a boil over high. Reduce heat to medium, and simmer until stock has a light shrimp flavor, about 1 hour. Pour through a fine wire-mesh strainer or a colander lined with cheesecloth into a large bowl. Discard solids. Set Shellfish Stock aside.

2 Prepare the Gumbo: Heat oil in a large Dutch oven over medium-high until shimmering. Whisk in flour; reduce heat to medium, and cook, stirring often with a wooden spoon, until roux is the color of peanut butter, 9 to 10 minutes. Reduce heat to medium-low; cook, stirring constantly, until roux is the color of melted milk chocolate (dark brown), about 12 minutes.

3 Carefully stir in onion, celery, bell peppers, garlic, Creole seasoning, filé powder, and hot sauce until coated (roux may splatter). Slowly whisk in prepared Shellfish Stock. Add bay leaves. Bring to a boil over high. Reduce heat to medium, and simmer, stirring and scraping bottom of Dutch oven occasionally with a wooden spoon, until gumbo has thickened and you can no longer taste the flour, about 1 hour, skimming and discarding fat from surface as needed. Stir in salt.

4 Stir in shrimp, oysters, and crabmeat, and cook, stirring occasionally, until shrimp is cooked through, 3 to 4 minutes. Serve gumbo over hot cooked rice, and garnish with scallions.

WINTER SALADS

HEARTY GREENS, JEWEL-TONE ROOTS AND
FRUITS, AND TOOTHSOME GRAINS COLLIDE IN
THESE SALADS THAT DESERVE A STARRING ROLE
ON YOUR TABLE THIS HOLIDAY SEASON.

Shaved Beet Salad with Herbs and Ricotta Salata

SERVES **8** HANDS-ON **20 MINUTES**
TOTAL **1 HOUR, 20 MINUTES**

Earthy beets, bright herbs, and salty cheese star in this salad dressed in holiday color. Ricotta salata is an aged cheese made from sheep's milk whey. If you cannot find it, feta is a worthy substitute.

6 tablespoons extra-virgin olive oil
4 tablespoons Champagne vinegar
2 teaspoons fresh lemon juice (from 1 lemon)
1 teaspoon kosher salt
½ teaspoon black pepper
6 medium-size red beets (2 pounds)
2 ounces ricotta salata cheese, crumbled (about ½ cup)
¼ cup torn fresh basil
¼ cup torn fresh mint

1 Whisk together oil, vinegar, lemon juice, salt, and pepper in a small bowl until blended. Reserve half of vinaigrette to dress salad. Set remaining vinaigrette aside.

2 Peel beets, and shave very thinly (⅛-inch thick) with a chef's knife or mandoline; place beets in a large bowl. Add remaining vinaigrette, and toss to combine; marinate at room temperature 1 hour.

3 Drain beets, discarding marinade. Place beets in a single layer on a platter; drizzle with reserved vinaigrette. Top with crumbled cheese, and sprinkle with basil and mint; serve immediately.

Apple Salad with Celery, Goat Cheese, and Crispy Leeks

SERVES **8** HANDS-ON **20 MINUTES** TOTAL **25 MINUTES**

This salad is a symphony of seasonal flavor. Celery complements sweet-tart apple while the crunch of the fried leeks plays off the creamy goat cheese.

Canola oil
3 small leeks (white and light green parts only), cut into thin, 2-inch-long pieces (2 cups)
2 tablespoons apple cider vinegar
½ tablespoon honey
1 teaspoon minced shallot (from 1 small shallot)
½ teaspoon kosher salt
¼ teaspoon black pepper
¼ cup olive oil
3 Fuji or Gala apples, thinly sliced (about 6 cups sliced)
2 tablespoons fresh lemon juice (from 1 lemon)
1 (5-ounce) package mixed fresh greens
4 celery stalks, thinly sliced diagonally (about 2 cups chopped)
½ cup toasted pecans, chopped
4 ounces goat cheese, crumbled

1 Pour oil to depth of 1 inch into a medium-size heavy saucepan; heat over medium-high to 350°F. Fry leeks, in 3 batches, until golden brown, about 30 seconds. Using slotted spoon, transfer fried leeks to paper towels to drain.

2 Whisk together vinegar, honey, shallot, salt, and pepper in a small bowl; add oil in a slow, steady stream, whisking constantly until smooth. Set vinaigrette aside.

3 Toss apples with lemon juice in a large bowl; let stand 30 seconds. Add mixed greens, celery, pecans, and vinaigrette, tossing until well coated. Transfer to a serving platter or bowl, and sprinkle with goat cheese and fried leeks. Serve immediately.

Farro, Sweet Potato, and Kale Salad with Lemon-Maple Vinaigrette

Farro is a protein- and fiber-rich whole grain that has a nutty flavor and chewy texture. It absorbs the flavors of whatever it is combined with, making it a wonderful addition to soups, pilafs, and salads.

1 Preheat oven to 400°F. Toss sweet potatoes with oil and chili powder on a large rimmed baking sheet. Bake in preheated oven until tender and lightly browned, 30 to 40 minutes.

2 Meanwhile, cook farro according to package directions. Drain; cool 20 minutes.

3 Place kale in a large bowl; add 2 tablespoons of the Lemon-Maple Vinaigrette, and massage into kale. Let stand 5 minutes. Add sweet potatoes, farro, cranberries, parsley, and 4 to 6 tablespoons of the Lemon-Maple Vinaigrette, stirring until well combined and coated. Serve immediately with remaining vinaigrette.

Lemon-Maple Vinaigrette

Whisk together **⅓ cup extra-virgin olive oil, ¼ cup fresh lemon juice, 1 tablespoon maple syrup, 1 tablespoon whole-grain mustard, ½ teaspoon kosher salt,** and **⅛ teaspoon black pepper** in a medium bowl. Cover and chill until ready to use. MAKES **1 CUP**

SERVES **10**
HANDS-ON **20 MINUTES**
TOTAL **1 HOUR, INCLUDING VINAIGRETTE**

---

2 medium-size sweet potatoes, cut into 1-inch cubes (about 3 cups)

2 tablespoons olive oil

1 teaspoon chili powder

1 cup uncooked pearled farro, rinsed

2 cups packed finely chopped lacinato kale (from 1 [8-ounce] bunch)

Lemon-Maple Vinaigrette (at left)

¼ cup sweetened dried cranberries

¼ cup chopped fresh flat-leaf parsley

Cool-Season Salad Swaps

ARUGULA + DANDELION
These strongly flavored greens may be used interchangeably. Arugula has a peppery quality, while dandelion greens lean toward pleasingly bitter. Choose young tender leaves of both for best flavor.

RED & GREEN ENDIVE + RADICCHIO
Tight heads of endive and the more open, compact heads of radicchio are bitter greens in the chicory family. They may be used relatively interchangeably. Temper the bitter bite of these greens with sweet flavor notes like balsamic vinegar, honey, maple syrup, or fruit. Grilling is another way to mellow the flavor.

MÂCHE + BUTTER LETTUCE
Mâche, also called corn salad or lamb's lettuce, grows as a rosette of tender leaves that are similar in appearance to watercress, though not as peppery in flavor. Mâche has vegetal flavor with subtle citrusy notes. Torn hearts of butter lettuce are an ideal substitute.

KALE + SWISS CHARD
Considered worthy substitutes for one another in most recipes, Swiss chard has an earthy flavor similar to beet greens while kale has a somewhat grassy flavor. Both are nutritional powerhouses. Kale is richer in vitamins A and C than most greens, but chard boasts considerably more iron than kale.

Cherry, Gorgonzola, and Arugula Salad

SERVES 8 HANDS-ON **10 MINUTES** TOTAL **10 MINUTES**

Fresh cherries aren't readily available in winter, but you may find them imported from warmer climates. If you cannot find fresh cherries, use frozen pitted cherries that have been thawed and drained thoroughly on a layer of paper towels. Alternatively, use dried tart cherries that have been reconstituted in hot water for about 5 minutes.

2 (5-ounce) packages baby arugula
20 fresh cherries, pitted and halved (1 ⅓ cups pitted, halved cherries)
¼ cup coarsely chopped fresh tarragon
½ cup toasted sliced almonds
¼ cup olive oil
3 tablespoons white balsamic vinegar
½ teaspoon kosher salt
¼ teaspoon black pepper
4 ounces Gorgonzola cheese, crumbled (about 1 cup)

Toss together arugula, cherries, tarragon, and ¼ cup of the almonds in a large bowl. Whisk together olive oil, vinegar, salt, and pepper in a small bowl; add to arugula mixture, and toss to combine. Arrange on a platter; sprinkle with cheese and remaining ¼ cup sliced almonds.

Roasted Mushroom Salad

SERVES 8 HANDS-ON **20 MINUTES** TOTAL **1 HOUR**

The meaty, earthy quality of a medley of mushrooms makes this a salad even the staunchest of carnivores will love.

¼ cup finely chopped shallots (from 3 small shallots)
¼ cup sherry vinegar
2 tablespoons chopped fresh flat-leaf parsley
2 teaspoons fresh thyme leaves
2 teaspoons honey
1 ½ teaspoons kosher salt
1 teaspoon black pepper
½ cup extra-virgin olive oil
8 ounces whole fresh portobello mushrooms, stemmed and mushrooms cut into ½-inch wedges
8 ounces fresh shiitake mushrooms, stems removed
8 ounces fresh cremini mushrooms, stems trimmed (halved if large)
8 ounces fresh oyster mushrooms, stems trimmed (halved if large)
8 ounces fresh baby spinach (8 cups)
1 cup thinly shaved fennel (from 1 [1-pound] bulb)
1 ½ ounces Parmigiano-Reggiano cheese, shaved (about ⅔ cup)

1 Preheat oven to 400°F. Whisk together shallots, vinegar, parsley, thyme, honey, salt, and pepper in a medium bowl. Add oil in a slow, steady stream, whisking constantly until smooth. Transfer half of vinaigrette to a large bowl, and reserve. Add mushrooms to remaining vinaigrette, and toss to coat; let stand 5 minutes.

2 Spread mushroom mixture in a single layer on a rimmed baking sheet. Roast in preheated oven until mushrooms are golden brown and crisp on the edges, 40 to 50 minutes, stirring after 20 minutes.

3 Transfer mushrooms to reserved vinaigrette in large bowl, and toss to coat. Add spinach, fennel, and cheese, and toss to combine. Transfer to a platter, and serve immediately.

Endive, Radish, and Fennel Salad with Cider Vinaigrette and Pomegranate

SERVES **8** HANDS-ON **15 MINUTES** TOTAL **15 MINUTES**

If you love a crunchy salad, look no further. Endive, fennel, and radish bring elements of bitter, sweet, and spicy for a crisp and complex side salad.

3 tablespoons apple cider vinegar
2 teaspoons minced shallot (from 1 small shallot)
1 teaspoon Dijon mustard
1 teaspoon honey
½ teaspoon kosher salt
¼ teaspoon black pepper
6 tablespoons olive oil

6 heads Belgian endive, halved lengthwise, cut crosswise into ½-inch pieces (5 cups pieces)
1 cup thinly sliced radishes (from 4 radishes)
2 cups thinly sliced fennel
2 tablespoons pomegranate arils
1 tablespoon thinly sliced fresh chives

1 Whisk together vinegar, shallot, mustard, honey, salt, and pepper in a small bowl. Add oil in a slow, steady stream, whisking constantly until smooth. Set vinaigrette aside.

2 Combine endive, radishes, and fennel in a large serving bowl. Drizzle with vinaigrette, tossing to coat. Sprinkle with pomegranate arils and chives; serve immediately.

Cauliflower Salad with Mâche, Hazelnut Vinaigrette, and Gruyère

SERVES **8** HANDS-ON **20 MINUTES** TOTAL **55 MINUTES**

Riced, mashed, or rolled into pizza crust, cauliflower gets star billing these days. This salad is a reminder of the perfectly presentable floret, whose nooks and crannies seem tailor-made for a nutty vinaigrette.

6 cups fresh cauliflower florets (from 2 small heads or 3 [10-ounce] packages florets)
1 cup thinly sliced yellow bell pepper (from 1 [6-ounce] pepper)
½ cup thinly sliced red onion (from 1 [4-ounce] onion)
2 tablespoons red wine vinegar
2 teaspoons Dijon mustard

1 tablespoon fresh lemon juice (from 1 lemon)
1 teaspoon kosher salt
¼ teaspoon black pepper
¼ cup hazelnut oil
8 ounces Gruyère cheese, cut into ¼-inch cubes (1¼ cups)
2 cups fresh mâche or arugula (from 1 [5-ounce] package)
¼ cup chopped toasted hazelnuts

1 Place a steamer basket in a large saucepan; add water to pan up to but not touching bottom of basket. Bring water to a boil over high. Add cauliflower florets; cover and steam until just tender, about 5 minutes. Drain.

2 Transfer cauliflower to a large bowl. Add bell pepper and onion; toss to combine.

3 Whisk together vinegar, mustard, lemon juice, salt, and pepper in a small bowl. Add hazelnut oil in a slow, steady stream, whisking constantly until smooth. Pour vinegar mixture over cauliflower mixture; add cheese, and gently toss to combine. Let stand at room temperature at least 30 minutes or up to 1 hour. Add mâche, and toss to combine; sprinkle with hazelnuts. Serve immediately.

PARTY CASSEROLES

THE COVERED DISH IS A HOLIDAY HOST'S BEST
FRIEND. LAYERED, SCALLOPED, BAKED, OR GRATINÉED,
CASSEROLES EQUAL COMFORT FOOD, BUT THESE
INSPIRED RECIPES ARE ALSO GUARANTEED TO IMPRESS.

Grits-and-Greens Strata

Two favorite Southern ingredients—grits and greens—come together in this rustic, hearty casserole that is as perfect for brunch with friends as it is on the holiday table.

1 Prepare the Grits: Cook oil and ham in a large saucepan over medium-high, stirring often, until browned, 6 to 8 minutes. Transfer ham with a slotted spoon to a bowl, reserving drippings in pan. Set ham aside. Add milk, broth, salt, and garlic to reserved drippings in saucepan, and bring to a boil over medium-high. Whisk in grits, reduce heat to medium-low, and cook, whisking often, until grits are tender and creamy, about 25 to 30 minutes. Remove from heat. Stir in cheese, butter, and pepper until well blended. Spread mixture evenly in a rimmed baking sheet lined with parchment paper, and let stand at room temperature 30 minutes. Refrigerate until completely chilled, 1 ½ hours. Cut grits into 4-inch squares.

2 Meanwhile, prepare the Greens: Heat oil in a large stockpot or Dutch oven over medium-high. Add onions, and cook, stirring occasionally, until lightly caramelized, 8 to 10 minutes. Add collard greens and garlic, and cook, tossing with tongs to incorporate onions, until greens are slightly wilted, 2 to 3 minutes. Add broth, sugar, and salt, and bring to a boil over medium-high. Cover, reduce heat to medium-low, and simmer until tender, 40 to 45 minutes. Stir in vinegar and pepper.

3 Preheat the oven to 450°F. Grease a 13- x 9-inch baking dish with 2 tablespoons butter. Layer grits squares and Greens in prepared baking dish, using tongs or a slotted spoon to add Greens. Top with ham and 1 cup shredded cheese. Bake in preheated oven until golden, 15 to 20 minutes. Serve with hot sauce.

SERVES **10**
HANDS-ON **1 HOUR, 20 MINUTES**
TOTAL **4 HOURS, 20 MINUTES,
INCLUDING 1 HOUR, 30
MINUTES CHILLING**

GRITS

1 tablespoon olive oil

**1 cup diced country ham
(5 ½ ounces)**

4 cups whole milk

4 cups chicken broth

1 teaspoon kosher salt

**2 garlic cloves, minced (about
2 teaspoons)**

**2 cups uncooked stone-ground
grits**

**4 ounces Gouda cheese, shredded
(about 1 cup)**

**¼ cup (2 ounces) unsalted
butter, softened**

½ teaspoon black pepper

GREENS

2 tablespoons olive oil

**3 cups vertically sliced yellow
onions (from 2 onions)**

**2 (16-ounce) packages chopped
fresh collard greens (20 cups
chopped)**

**5 garlic cloves, sliced (about
5 teaspoons)**

1 cup chicken broth

2 teaspoons granulated sugar

1 teaspoon kosher salt

2 tablespoons red wine vinegar

½ teaspoon black pepper

ADDITIONAL INGREDIENTS

2 tablespoons unsalted butter

**4 ounces Gouda cheese, shredded
(about 1 cup)**

Hot sauce

Roasted Artichokes with Mushrooms and Parmesan

SERVES **8** HANDS-ON **30 MINUTES**
TOTAL **1 HOUR, 30 MINUTES**

This is a light and elegant side dish. Be sure to cook all of the liquid out of the mushrooms or you will have a mushy mess. A grapefruit spoon is the perfect tool to scoop out the hairy choke.

- **3 tablespoons unsalted butter**
- **8 ounces cremini mushrooms, chopped**
- **2 teaspoons chopped fresh rosemary**
- **1 teaspoon kosher salt**
- **½ teaspoon black pepper**
- **5 garlic cloves, minced**
- **2 teaspoons lemon zest, plus 9 tablespoons fresh juice (from 4 lemons, reserving lemon halves)**
- **2 cups (Japanese breadcrumbs)**
- **4 ounces Parmesan cheese, shredded (about 1 cup)**
- **4 ounces pecorino Romano, shredded (about 1 cup)**
- **⅓ cup olive oil**
- **2 tablespoons chopped fresh flat-leaf parsley**
- **8 fresh artichokes (8 ounces each)**
- **½ cup dry white wine**
- **1 cup water**

1 Preheat oven to 400°F. Melt butter in a large skillet over high; add mushrooms, and cook, stirring often, until lightly browned, 6 minutes. Add rosemary, salt, pepper, and garlic; cook, stirring often, until all liquid has evaporated, 2 minutes. Cool completely, about 20 minutes. Chop very finely.

2 Combine mushroom mixture, lemon zest, panko, cheeses, olive oil, and parsley in a large bowl.

3 Place artichokes in a separate large bowl, and add water to cover; stir in lemon juice. Remove 1 artichoke, and trim about 2 inches from top of artichoke. Cut stem from artichoke, and remove fuzzy thistle from bottom with a spoon; discard. Trim dark green layer and any leaves from base. Rub edges of leaves, especially cut ends, with reserved lemon halves, and return artichoke to lemon-water mixture. Repeat procedure with remaining artichokes, 1 at a time.

4 Remove 1 artichoke, leaving remaining artichokes in water. Separate leaves, and stuff breadcrumb mixture under leaves. Place artichoke, stem side down, in a 13- x 9-inch baking dish. Repeat procedure with remaining artichokes. Pour wine and 1 cup water into baking dish, and cover loosely with aluminum foil. Bake in preheated oven until tender and breadcrumb mixture is toasted, 45 minutes to 1 hour.

Scalloped Yams and Parsnips

SERVES **12** HANDS-ON **20 MINUTES**
TOTAL **1 HOUR, 20 MINUTES**

Think beyond the new potatoes and carrots. Earthy yams and distinctively sweet parsnips add interest to any meal and are a nice change of pace from the usual roasted roots.

- **2 tablespoons salted butter**
- **3 pounds parsnips, peeled and thinly sliced**
- **2 pounds yams, peeled and very thinly sliced**
- **8 ounces Gruyère cheese, shredded (about 2 cups)**
- **1½ tablespoons chopped fresh thyme**
- **2 teaspoons kosher salt**
- **1 teaspoon black pepper**
- **2 cups heavy cream**
- **1 tablespoon chopped fresh flat-leaf parsley**

1 Preheat oven to 375°F. Grease a 13- x 9-inch baking dish with butter. Arrange one-third of parsnip slices in a single layer in prepared baking dish; top with one-third of yam slices in a single layer. Sprinkle with one-third of cheese, thyme, salt, and pepper. Repeat parsnip and yam layers and sprinkling with cheese, thyme, salt, and pepper twice. Pour cream over layers.

2 Bake in preheated oven until vegetables are tender and top is browned, 50 minutes to 1 hour. Let stand 10 minutes. Sprinkle with parsley, and serve immediately.

Chicken Saltimbocca Casserole

Italian for "jumps in mouth," this casserole spin on the Italian classic saltimbocca—pounded veal or chicken rolled with prosciutto and sage—is as delicious as its name suggests.

1 Cook pasta according to package directions; drain. Heat oil in a large skillet over high. Sprinkle chicken with 1 ½ teaspoons of the salt and ¾ teaspoon of the pepper. Add chicken to skillet, and cook until browned on 1 side, 4 to 5 minutes. Turn chicken over, and cook until browned on other side, 3 to 4 minutes. Add wine, and bring to a boil. Reduce heat to medium-low, and simmer until a meat thermometer inserted into thickest part of chicken breast registers 155°F, 10 to 12 minutes. Transfer chicken to a cutting board, and let rest 10 minutes. Cut chicken into 1-inch pieces, reserving juices from cutting board. Place chicken and reserved juices in a large bowl. Preheat oven to 450°F.

2 Melt butter in a large saucepan over medium-high until foamy. Whisk in flour until smooth; cook, whisking constantly, until barely browned, about 2 minutes. Add milk, and bring to a boil, whisking often. Reduce heat to medium, and simmer, whisking often, until slightly thickened, about 5 minutes. Remove sauce from heat, and stir in 1 cup provolone cheese and remaining ¾ teaspoon salt and ½ teaspoon pepper.

3 Add cooked pasta, sauce, capers (if desired), zest, asparagus, and half of prosciutto to chicken, stirring until well blended. Spoon into a lightly greased 13- x 9-inch baking dish. Top with remaining 1 cup provolone and remaining half of prosciutto. Sprinkle with Parmesan and sage. Bake in preheated oven until bubbly, top is browned, and asparagus is tender, 15 to 20 minutes. Serve immediately with lemon wedges.

SERVES **10**
HANDS-ON **55 MINUTES**
TOTAL **1 HOUR, 10 MINUTES**

---

12 ounces uncooked penne pasta

3 tablespoons olive oil

4 boneless, skinless chicken breasts (2 ¼ pounds)

2 ¼ teaspoons kosher salt

1 ¼ teaspoons black pepper

¾ cup dry white wine

3 tablespoons unsalted butter

3 tablespoons all-purpose flour

3 cups whole milk

8 ounces provolone cheese, shredded (about 2 cups)

1 tablespoon drained capers (optional)

1 teaspoon lemon zest (from 1 lemon)

1 pound fresh asparagus, trimmed and cut into 2-inch lengths

6 ounces thinly sliced prosciutto, cut into ½-inch-wide slivers

2 ounces Parmesan cheese, grated (about ½ cup)

12 fresh sage leaves

Lemon wedges

Beef Bourguignon Pie

SERVES **10**
HANDS-ON **1 HOUR, 5 MINUTES**
TOTAL **3 HOURS, 5 MINUTES**

2 tablespoons olive oil

4 thick-cut bacon slices, coarsely chopped

3 pounds boneless chuck roast, trimmed, cut into (2-inch) cubes

3 cups halved cremini mushrooms (quartered if very large) (8 ounces)

1 pound carrots, diagonally sliced into 1-inch pieces

1 tablespoon chopped fresh thyme

4 garlic cloves, chopped (about 4 teaspoons)

1 tablespoon tomato paste

½ cup (4 ounces) brandy

3 cups full-bodied red wine (such as French Burgundy)

1 ¾ cups beef broth

3 cups frozen pearl onions, thawed (from 1 [14.4-ounce] package)

2 teaspoons kosher salt

1 teaspoon black pepper

2 tablespoons all-purpose flour

1 ½ pounds russet potatoes, peeled and cut into 1 ½-inch pieces

1 bay leaf

¼ cup (2 ounces) salted butter

2 tablespoons whole milk

1 tablespoon chopped fresh flat-leaf parsley

Beef braised in red wine—traditionally red Burgundy—is French country fare made famous by Julia Child. An ample dose of brandy adds complex flavor to the slow-simmered classic.

1 Cook oil and bacon in a large Dutch oven over medium, stirring occasionally, until bacon is crispy, 6 to 8 minutes. Transfer bacon with a slotted spoon to a large bowl, reserving drippings in Dutch oven. Increase heat to medium-high, and cook roast pieces, in batches, in reserved drippings, turning occasionally, until browned on all sides, 6 to 8 minutes per batch. Transfer roast pieces to bowl with bacon, reserving drippings in Dutch oven.

2 Add mushrooms to reserved drippings in Dutch oven; cook over medium-high, stirring occasionally, until browned and liquid has evaporated, 8 to 10 minutes; transfer mushrooms to bowl with bacon and roast pieces, reserving drippings in Dutch oven. Add carrots to reserved drippings in Dutch oven; cook, stirring occasionally, until lightly browned, 5 to 6 minutes. Add thyme and garlic; cook, stirring constantly, 1 minute. Add tomato paste, and cook, stirring constantly, 1 minute. Remove from heat, and stir in brandy. Cook over medium-high, stirring to loosen browned bits from bottom of Dutch oven, until almost all liquid has evaporated, 1 to 2 minutes. Add wine, 1 ½ cups of the broth, and onions; bring to a boil, stirring occasionally. Boil, stirring occasionally, until mixture thickens, 2 to 3 minutes. Stir in 1 teaspoon of the salt, and ½ teaspoon of the pepper. Whisk flour into remaining ¼ cup broth. Stir into mixture in Dutch oven. Return bacon, roast pieces, mushrooms, and any accumulated juices to Dutch oven. Cover, reduce heat to medium-low, and simmer until roast is very tender, 1 ¼ to 2 hours, stirring every 30 minutes.

3 Meanwhile, place potatoes and bay leaf in a large saucepan, and add water to cover. Bring to a boil over high; reduce heat to medium, and simmer until very tender, about 10 minutes. Drain potatoes, discarding bay leaf. Return potatoes to pan; add butter, milk, and remaining 1 teaspoon salt and ½ teaspoon pepper, and mash with a potato masher until smooth and fluffy.

4 Preheat broiler to high with oven rack 7 to 8 inches from heat. Place roast mixture in a lightly greased 3-quart ceramic baking dish. Dollop with mashed potatoes. Broil until lightly toasted, 3 to 4 minutes. Let stand 10 minutes. Sprinkle with parsley, and serve immediately.

Colcannon Gratin

This mashed potato and cabbage casserole has roots in Ireland, where it is often served on Halloween—like the King Cake of Mardi Gras with trinkets and coins hidden inside.

1 Melt 4 tablespoons butter in a large Dutch oven over medium-high until foamy. Add onions; stir well to coat. Cook, stirring often, until onions are just beginning to brown, 10 to 12 minutes. Reduce heat to medium-low, stir in ¾ teaspoon of the salt, and cook, stirring often, until onions are a light caramel color, 8 to 10 minutes. Remove from heat, and stir in whiskey and cabbage. Increase heat to medium-high, and cook, stirring occasionally, until cabbage is just wilted but still tender-crisp, 6 to 8 minutes.

2 Preheat oven to 375°F. Grease a 13- x 9-inch baking dish with remaining 2 tablespoons butter. Arrange a layer of russet potato slices in prepared baking dish; top with a layer of Yukon Gold potato slices. Spoon half of onion mixture over potatoes, and top with 1 ¼ cups of the cheese. Sprinkle with ¾ teaspoon of the salt and ½ teaspoon of the pepper. Repeat potato and onion layers. Pour cream over layers, and sprinkle with remaining ¾ teaspoon salt and ½ teaspoon pepper. Coat 1 side of a piece of aluminum foil with cooking spray, and place foil over baking dish, coated side down, to keep it from sticking.

3 Bake in the preheated oven until the potatoes are tender, 1 hour and 15 minutes to 1 hour and 30 minutes. Increase oven temperature to broil. Remove foil from dish, and sprinkle remaining 1 ¼ cups cheese evenly over casserole. Broil until golden brown, 2 to 3 minutes. Let stand 15 minutes before serving.

SERVES **12**
HANDS-ON **35 MINUTES**
TOTAL **2 HOURS, 5 MINUTES**

- **6 tablespoons (3 ounces) salted butter**
- **3 large onions, thinly sliced vertically (7 cups sliced)**
- **2 ¼ teaspoons kosher salt**
- **¼ cup (2 ounces) Irish whiskey**
- **4 cups thinly sliced cabbage (from 1 small head)**
- **2 pounds russet potatoes, peeled and very thinly sliced**
- **2 pounds Yukon Gold potatoes, peeled and very thinly sliced**
- **10 ounces Irish Cheddar cheese, shredded (about 2 ½ cups)**
- **1 teaspoon black pepper**
- **2 cups heavy cream**

Sizing Up Baking Dishes and Pans

13- X 9-INCH BAKING DISH	12 TO 15 CUPS
10- X 4-INCH TUBE PAN	16 CUPS
10- X 3 ½-INCH BUNDT PAN	12 CUPS
9- X 3-INCH TUBE PAN	9 CUPS
9- X 3-INCH BUNDT PAN	9 CUPS
11- X 7-INCH BAKING DISH	8 CUPS
8-INCH SQUARE BAKING DISH	8 CUPS
9- X 5-INCH LOAF PAN	8 CUPS
9-INCH DEEP DISH PIE PAN	6 TO 8 CUPS
9- X 1 ½-INCH CAKE PAN	6 CUPS
7 ½- X 3-INCH BUNDT PAN	6 CUPS
9- X 1 ½-INCH PIE PAN	5 CUPS
8- X 1 ½-INCH CAKE PAN	4 TO 5 CUPS
8- X 4-INCH LOAF PAN	4 CUPS

Brussels Sprout Gratin

SERVES **8**
HANDS-ON **30 MINUTES**
TOTAL **40 MINUTES**

---

4 thick-cut bacon slices, chopped

2 tablespoons olive oil

1 ¹/₂ pounds fresh Brussels sprouts, trimmed and halved lengthwise

3 shallots, thinly sliced

2 garlic cloves, thinly sliced (about 2 teaspoons)

1 teaspoon caraway seeds

¹/₂ cup dry white wine

³/₄ teaspoon kosher salt

1 teaspoon black pepper

¹/₄ teaspoon freshly grated nutmeg

3 ounces fontina cheese, shredded (about ³/₄ cup)

³/₄ cup heavy cream

1 cup panko (Japanese-style breadcrumbs)

¹/₄ cup melted salted butter

Even those who typically turn their noses up at Brussels sprouts won't be able to resist this gratin layered with smoky bacon and cheese and finished with a layer of crisp, buttery crumbs.

1 Preheat oven to 425°F. Cook bacon and oil in a large skillet over medium, stirring occasionally, until bacon is beginning to crisp. Transfer bacon with a slotted spoon to paper towels to drain, reserving drippings in skillet. Increase heat to medium-high, and cook Brussels sprouts and shallots in reserved drippings, stirring occasionally, until lightly browned, 2 to 3 minutes. Add garlic and caraway seeds; cook, stirring often, 1 minute. Add wine; bring to a boil. Cover, reduce heat to medium-low, and simmer until tender-crisp, 8 to 9 minutes. Remove from heat. Transfer to a large bowl, and toss with salt, pepper, and nutmeg. Cool slightly, about 5 minutes. Stir in cheese and chopped bacon.

2 Spoon mixture into a lightly greased 13- x 9-inch baking dish. Pour cream over mixture. Toss panko with butter in a medium bowl; sprinkle panko mixture evenly over casserole. Bake in preheated oven until golden brown and bubbly, 10 to 12 minutes.

FRESH BAKED

THE AROMA OF FRESH BAKED BREAD BECKONS LIKE FEW THINGS DO, TRANSPORTING US BACK TO HOME, HEARTH, AND HOLIDAY. CUE UP THE CHRISTMAS CAROLS AND CREATE A LITTLE BAKERY MAGIC TO ENJOY AND SHARE.

Rustic Italian Loaf

SERVES **12**
HANDS-ON **20 MINUTES**
TOTAL **3 HOURS, 30 MINUTES**

---

1 ½ teaspoons active dry yeast (from 1 packet)

1 teaspoon granulated sugar

1 cup warm water (100°F to 110°F)

2 tablespoons extra-virgin olive oil

2 ¾ cups (about 11 ¾ ounces) bread flour

1 tablespoon finely chopped fresh rosemary, plus more for garnish

1 ¼ teaspoons kosher salt

1 large egg, beaten

Coarse sea salt (optional)

If you are a novice baker, this bread recipe is an easy way to hone your skills. It yields a terrific sandwich bread or perfect slice for toasting and slathering with softened, salted butter.

1 Combine yeast, sugar, and water in a small bowl. Let stand until foamy, about 5 minutes. Combine yeast mixture and olive oil in the bowl of a heavy-duty stand mixer fitted with a dough hook. Gradually add flour, rosemary, and kosher salt, beating on low speed until a soft dough forms, 5 to 7 minutes.

2 Increase speed to medium, and beat until dough is smooth and elastic, about 5 minutes.

3 Transfer dough to a lightly greased bowl, turning to grease top; cover and let rise in a warm place (80°F to 85°F), free from drafts, until doubled in size, 45 minutes to 1 hour.

4 Preheat oven to 400°F. Turn dough out onto a lightly floured surface. Shape into a 12-inch oblong loaf, and place on a parchment paper-lined baking sheet. Cover loosely with plastic wrap, and let rise in a warm place (80°F to 85°F) until increased in size, 30 to 45 minutes. Gently brush loaf with beaten egg, and sprinkle with additional finely chopped fresh rosemary and, if desired, coarse sea salt. Cut 3 (¼-inch-deep) slits across top of loaf. Bake in preheated oven until golden brown, about 30 minutes. Transfer loaf to a wire rack to cool completely, about 1 hour.

For Good Measure

Measuring dry ingredients accurately is one of the keys to mastering the perfect loaf. Flour can be densely packed or overly fluffed up, depending on how it is stored. An extra half ounce of flour can be the difference between a loaf that's light and tender or dense as a brick.

The foolproof way to measure dry ingredients is by weight (ounces or grams) with a kitchen scale. One cup of all-purpose flour weighs 120 grams or 4 ¼ ounces. There are plenty of simple, inexpensive kitchen scales available, but if you can't squeeze another gadget into your kitchen, measure dry ingredients by volume (cups) with a regular old measuring cup. Here's how to do it accurately:

1. FLUFF UP THE FLOUR
Use a spoon to gently stir up the flour. This is especially important if you're scooping the flour directly from the bag, where it tends to get tightly packed.

2. SPOON IT INTO A MEASURING CUP
Instead of scooping the flour directly from the bag or container, use a spoon to fill the measuring cup, mounding it a bit on top.

3. LEVEL IT OFF
Draw the straight edge of a knife or spatula across the top of the measuring cup to level it off and remove excess flour.

Pullman Loaf

SERVES **8** HANDS-ON **55 MINUTES**
TOTAL **6 HOURS**

This is a light and buttery loaf with a tender crumb. You are sure to wow your guests and no one needs to know how very simple this bread is to make.

¼ cup water
3 cups (about 12 ¾ ounces) bread flour
1 cup whole milk
3 tablespoons granulated sugar
2 teaspoons instant or quick-rising yeast (such as Fleischmann's RapidRise)(from 1 packet)
1 ¼ teaspoons kosher salt
1 large egg, beaten
4 tablespoons unsalted butter, softened and cut into ½-inch pieces
1 tablespoon unsalted butter, melted

1 Whisk together water, ¼ cup of the flour, and ½ cup of the milk in a small saucepan until smooth. Cook over medium-low, stirring often, until thickened, 4 to 6 minutes. Transfer mixture to a small bowl. Cover with plastic wrap, pressing wrap directly onto surface of mixture, and let cool to room temperature, at least 1 hour.

2 Combine sugar, yeast, salt, and the remaining 2 ¾ cups flour in the bowl of a heavy-duty stand mixer fitted with dough hook. Beat on low speed until combined. Add egg, cooked flour mixture, and remaining ½ cup milk. Beat on low speed until well blended, about 8 to 10 minutes. With mixer running on low speed, gradually add 4 tablespoons softened butter, beating until dough is smooth and tacky, about 15 minutes. Using floured hands, transfer dough to a lightly greased bowl, turning to grease top. Cover and let rise in a warm place (80°F to 85°F), free from drafts, until doubled in size, about 1 ½ hours.

3 Turn dough out onto a lightly floured surface. Shape into an 8-inch oblong loaf, and place in a lightly greased 8- x 4-inch loaf pan. Cover loosely with plastic wrap, and let rise in a warm place (80°F to 85°F), free from drafts, until doubled in size, 40 to 50 minutes. Preheat oven to 375°F. Cut a ¼-inch-deep slit lengthwise along top of loaf, beginning and ending 1 ½ inches from either end. Bake in preheated oven until golden brown, 30 to 35 minutes. Remove from oven, and brush 1 tablespoon melted butter over top of loaf. Cool in pan on a wire rack 10 minutes. Remove loaf from pan, and cool on wire rack at least 1 hour before serving.

Braided Cardamom Bread

SERVES **24** HANDS-ON **25 MINUTES**
TOTAL **3 HOURS, 25 MINUTES**

Be sure to use instant yeast, not active dry. This makes the best French toast or bread pudding.

⅔ cup granulated sugar
1 ½ tablespoons instant yeast (from 2 packets)
1 tablespoon kosher salt
2 teaspoons orange zest
1 ½ teaspoons ground cardamom
8 ¼ cups all-purpose flour
⅔ cup canola oil
1 ¼ cups very warm water (125°F to 135°F)
5 large eggs
1 teaspoon tap water
2 tablespoons turbinado sugar

1 Combine first 5 ingredients and 4 ¾ cups of the flour in the bowl of a stand mixer fitted with paddle attachment. Beat on low to combine. Add oil, beating on low, until mixture resembles small peas, about 1 minute. Gradually add the warm water, beating on medium speed for 2 minutes.

2 Add 4 eggs, 1 at a time, beating well after each addition. Scrape down sides of bowl, as needed. Replace paddle attachment with the dough hook. Gradually add remaining 3 ½ cups flour, beating on medium-low until dough is smooth and elastic, 6 to 8 minutes. Dough will be sticky. Transfer to a greased bowl, turning to grease top; cover. Let rise in a warm place (80°F to 85°F) until doubled in size, about 1 hour.

3 Turn dough out onto a floured surface. Divide in half. Cover 1 half with a towel; set aside. Divide remaining half into 4 equal pieces. Roll each piece into a 14-inch log. Pinch ends of logs together at 1 end to seal. Braid dough by starting with the strand on the left and moving it to the right over 2 strands and then back to the left under 1 strand. Take the right strand, and move it to the left over 2 strands and then move it back to the right under 1 strand. Repeat braiding process until loaf is complete. (Divide dough into 3 strands for a simpler braid, if desired.) Pinch loose end to seal. Transfer to a parchment-lined baking sheet. Tuck both ends under. Repeat process with remaining dough on a second baking sheet.

4 Whisk together 1 teaspoon water and the remaining egg in a small bowl. Brush braids with egg wash. Reserve remaining mixture. Cover braids loosely with greased plastic wrap. Let rise in a warm place (80°F to 85°F) until doubled, 1 ½ hours. Preheat the oven to 375°F. Uncover loaves. Brush again with reserved egg wash. Sprinkle with turbinado sugar. Bake in the oven until deep golden brown, 28 to 30 minutes. Transfer to a wire rack to cool completely.

Black Pepper–Gruyère Biscuits

MAKES **1 DOZEN** HANDS-ON **20 MINUTES**
TOTAL **45 MINUTES**

Spelt flour is becoming widely available. Look for Bob's Red Mill and Arrowhead Mills brands. The process of patting or rolling out the dough into a rectangle and then folding and repeating creates an undeniably flaky, buttery layered biscuit.

3 ½ cups (about 14 ⅞ ounces) all-purpose flour
1 ½ tablespoons granulated sugar
2 teaspoons kosher salt
1 tablespoon baking powder
2 teaspoons black pepper
½ teaspoon baking soda

1 ¼ cups (10 ounces) salted butter, chilled and cut into ½-inch pieces
2 ounces Gruyère cheese, finely grated (about ¾ cup)
1 ¼ cups whole buttermilk
2 tablespoons unsalted butter, melted

1 Preheat oven to 425°F. Combine flour, sugar, salt, baking powder, black pepper, and baking soda in a large bowl. Using a pastry blender, cut 1 ¼ cups salted butter into flour mixture until mixture resembles small peas. Stir in cheese. Add buttermilk, stirring with a fork until a shaggy dough forms.

2 Transfer dough to a lightly floured surface. Gently roll dough into a 1-inch-thick rectangle, and fold in half so short ends meet. Repeat rolling and folding 3 more times. Roll dough into a 6- x 8-inch rectangle (about 1 inch thick), and cut into 12 (2-inch) squares. Place biscuits 2 inches apart on a parchment paper-lined baking sheet.

3 Freeze until cold, about 10 minutes. Bake in preheated oven until golden brown, about 15 to 17 minutes. Brush biscuits with 2 tablespoons melted unsalted butter.

VARIATION

Honey-Butter Spelt Biscuits

Omit black pepper and Gruyère cheese. Prepare recipe as directed, substituting **¾ cup (about 3 ⅜ ounces) spelt flour** for ¾ cup (about 3 ¼ ounces) of the all-purpose flour and stirring **1 tablespoon honey** into 2 tablespoons melted unsalted butter before brushing over baked biscuits. MAKES **1 DOZEN**

Monkey Bread Muffins

MAKES **1 DOZEN** HANDS-ON **30 MINUTES**
TOTAL **2 HOURS**

A Christmas morning treat that your whole family will love. These are ooey-gooey delicious with the taste of fresh baked yeast bread and the decadence of a sticky bun rolled into one.

1 (1-pound, 9-ounce) package frozen yeast roll dough (24 count) (such as Bridgford Parkerhouse Style Rolls)
¼ cup light corn syrup
2 tablespoons heavy cream
¼ teaspoon table salt

1 cup (8 ounces) unsalted butter, melted
1 cup packed dark brown sugar
¾ cup granulated sugar
1 cup coarsely chopped toasted pecans
2 teaspoons ground cinnamon

1 Thaw roll dough according to package directions; cut rolls in half. Lightly grease 2 (6-cup) jumbo muffin pans.

2 Combine corn syrup, heavy cream, salt, ½ cup butter, ½ cup brown sugar, and ¼ cup granulated sugar in a medium bowl. Divide mixture evenly between muffin cups (about 1 ½ tablespoons each). Sprinkle cups evenly with pecans (about 1 tablespoon each).

3 Stir together cinnamon and remaining ½ cup each brown and granulated sugars in a small bowl. Dip each roll half in remaining ½ cup butter; dredge in cinnamon mixture. Place 4 coated roll halves on pecans in each muffin cup. Cover pans loosely with plastic wrap, and let rise in a warm place (80°F to 85°F), free from drafts, until doubled in size, about 1 hour.

4 Preheat oven to 325°F. Uncover muffins, and bake in preheated oven until golden brown, 20 to 25 minutes. Let cool in pans on wire rack 5 minutes. Invert muffins onto a serving platter, and serve immediately.

Blackberry Ebleskiver

SERVES **8** HANDS-ON **35 MINUTES** TOTAL **35 MINUTES**

Ebleskiver means "apples" in Danish, which is thought to refer to the shape of this sugar-dusted bread. You will need an Ebleskiver pan for this recipe, which is easily found online or in fine kitchen stores. Similar to beignets, these are terrific with coffee.

1 ¼ cups (5 ⅜ ounces) all-purpose flour
3 tablespoons granulated sugar
2 teaspoons baking powder
¼ teaspoon ground ginger
¼ teaspoon table salt

1 large egg, beaten
1 cup whole milk
2 tablespoons melted salted butter, plus more for pan
16 teaspoons seedless blackberry jam
Powdered sugar

1 Whisk together flour, granulated sugar, baking powder, ginger, and salt in a medium bowl until combined. In a separate medium bowl, stir together egg, milk, and butter until blended. Add egg mixture to flour mixture, stirring just until combined. (Batter should be lumpy. Do not overmix.)

2 Heat an ebleskiver pan over medium-low until hot. Brush pan lightly with butter, and drop 1 tablespoon of batter into each of 8 indentations in hot pan. Top each with 1 teaspoon blackberry jam, and spoon ½ tablespoon batter over each. Cook until bottoms are golden brown, about 4 minutes. Turn over, and cook until ebleskiver are completely golden brown, about 3 minutes. Transfer to a serving plate. Sprinkle with powdered sugar. Repeat procedure with remaining batter and blackberry jam.

Lemon-Pistachio Loaf

SERVES **8** HANDS-ON **20 MINUTES**
TOTAL **2 HOURS, 15 MINUTES**

Citrus and pistachios offer a nice change of pace from the usual holiday loaf.

1 ¾ cups raw shelled pistachios
1 ¼ cups (about 5 ⅜ ounces) all-purpose flour
1 teaspoon baking powder
¼ teaspoon baking soda
¾ teaspoon kosher salt
½ cup (4 ounces) unsalted butter, softened

1 cup granulated sugar
2 large eggs
½ cup whole buttermilk
1 tablespoon lemon zest, plus ¼ cup plus 1 to 2 teaspoons fresh juice
1 teaspoon vanilla extract
1 cup (about 4 ounces) powdered sugar

1 Preheat oven to 350°F. Grease and flour an 8- x 4-inch loaf pan. Process 1 cup pistachios in a food processor until finely chopped. Coarsely chop remaining ¾ cup pistachios; set aside. Whisk together flour, baking powder, baking soda, salt, and the finely chopped pistachios in a medium bowl.

2 Beat butter and 1 cup granulated sugar with an electric mixer on medium-high until light and fluffy, 4 minutes. Add eggs, 1 at a time, beating after each. Add flour mixture to butter mixture alternately with buttermilk. Beat on low until blended after each addition. Stir in zest, vanilla, the coarsely chopped pistachios, and 3 tablespoons of the lemon juice.

3 Spoon batter into prepared loaf pan; smooth top. Bake until golden brown and a wooden pick inserted in center comes out clean, 40 to 50 minutes. Cool in pan on wire rack 10 minutes. Remove loaf from pan to wire rack. Cool completely, about 1 hour.

4 Whisk together 1 cup powdered sugar and 1 tablespoon lemon juice until smooth, adding remaining 1 to 2 teaspoons juice, if needed, for desired consistency. Drizzle over cooled loaf.

VARIATION

Orange-Pistachio Loaf

Prepare recipe as directed, substituting **orange zest** for lemon zest and **orange juice** for lemon juice and stirring **¾ teaspoon ground cardamom** into batter with coarsely chopped pistachios in Step 2. SERVES **8**

Linzertorte Layer Cake

SERVES **8 TO 12** HANDS-ON **55 MINUTES**
TOTAL **4 HOURS, INCLUDING BUTTERCREAM AND CHILLING**

This is a very light cake, so you won't feel overstuffed having a slice after Christmas dinner. Raspberry jam gives this a nice Christmas feel.

3 cups (11 1/4 ounces) bleached cake flour (such as Swans Down)	7 large egg whites, at room temperature
3/4 cup (2 5/8 ounces) almond flour	1 cup water
4 teaspoons baking powder	2 teaspoons vanilla extract
1 teaspoon table salt	1/2 teaspoon almond extract
1 teaspoon ground cinnamon	Brown Sugar Buttercream (recipe follows)
1 1/4 cups (10 ounces) unsalted butter, softened	3/4 cup seedless raspberry jam
2 1/4 cups granulated sugar	1 cup sliced almonds, toasted

1 Preheat oven to 350°F. Spray 4 (8-inch) round cake pans with baking spray. Place an 8-inch parchment paper circle in the bottom of each pan. Whisk together cake flour, almond flour, baking powder, salt, and cinnamon in a medium bowl. Set aside.

2 Beat butter and sugar with an electric mixer on medium until light and fluffy, about 5 minutes. Gradually add egg whites, beating well after each addition. Gradually add flour mixture to butter mixture alternately with water, beginning and ending with flour mixture. Beat on medium speed just until blended after each addition. Stir in extracts. Divide batter evenly among prepared cake pans.

3 Bake until a wooden pick inserted in center comes out clean, 22 to 25 minutes. Cool in pans on wire racks 10 minutes; remove from pans to wire racks, and cool completely, about 30 minutes.

4 Place 1 cake layer on a cake plate. Spoon 1 cup Brown Sugar Buttercream into a ziplock plastic freezer bag. Snip 1 corner of bag to make a small hole. Pipe a ring of frosting around cake layer just inside the top edge. Spread cake layer with about 1/4 cup raspberry jam, spreading to edge of piped frosting. Repeat twice, top with remaining cake layer, and spread a thin layer of frosting around sides of cake. Chill, uncovered, 2 hours. Press plastic wrap directly onto surface of remaining frosting; let stand at room temperature while cake chills.

5 Spread remaining frosting on top and sides of chilled cake, piping a basket weave or lattice design on top, if desired. Garnish top edge of cake with almonds.

Brown Sugar Buttercream

1 1/2 cups (12 ounces) unsalted butter, softened	5 cups (about 20 ounces) powdered sugar
1/2 cup packed light brown sugar	1 teaspoon vanilla extract
	2 tablespoons heavy cream

Beat butter and brown sugar with an electric mixer on medium speed until creamy, about 4 minutes. Reduce speed to low, and gradually add powdered sugar, beating until smooth and scraping down sides of bowl as needed, about 2 minutes. Beat in vanilla. With mixer running on medium speed, gradually add cream, beating until fluffy and spreadable, about 30 seconds. Makes 3 cups

Individual Red Berry Pavlovas

SERVES **12** HANDS-ON **30 MINUTES**
TOTAL **18 HOURS, INCLUDING 8 HOURS CHILLING AND 8 HOURS STANDING**

Crunchy on the outside and soft on the inside, the sugared cranberries are pretty and add a sweet-tart element.

1 cup pure maple syrup	1/4 teaspoon cream of tartar
2 cups fresh cranberries (about 14 ounces)	1/8 teaspoon table salt
1 1/2 tablespoons cornstarch	1 teaspoon vanilla extract
1 3/4 cups granulated sugar	1 cup superfine sugar
6 large egg whites, at room temperature	1 1/2 cups heavy cream
	1 cup fresh raspberries (6 ounces)
	Fresh mint leaves

1 Place maple syrup in a medium-size microwavable bowl. Microwave on HIGH until warm, about 1 minute. Stir in cranberries. Cover and chill 8 hours or up to overnight.

2 Preheat oven to 225°F. Whisk together cornstarch and 1 1/2 cups of the granulated sugar in a medium bowl; set aside. Beat egg whites in the bowl of a heavy-duty stand mixer fitted with whisk attachment on medium speed until foamy, about 1 minute. Add cream of tartar and salt, beating until blended. Add granulated sugar mixture, 2 tablespoons at a time, beating on medium-high speed until mixture is glossy and stiff peaks form, about 4 minutes. Beat in vanilla.

3 Spoon or pipe egg white mixture into 12 (4-inch) mounds on 2 parchment paper-lined baking sheets. Use the back of a spoon to flatten mounds slightly and create an indentation in the center of each. Bake until a crust has formed and Pavlovas are no longer sticky, about 1 ½ hours. Turn oven off and do not open door; let meringues stand in oven, with door closed, 8 to 12 hours.

4 Meanwhile, drain cranberries in a colander for 15 minutes, reserving maple syrup for another use. Place superfine sugar in a medium bowl. Toss cranberries with superfine sugar, in batches, until completely coated; transfer to a parchment paper-lined baking sheet to dry, about 2 hours.

5 Combine heavy cream and remaining ¼ cup granulated sugar in the bowl of a heavy-duty stand mixer fitted with whisk attachment. Beat on medium-high speed until soft peaks form, about 3 minutes. To serve, spoon raspberries and cranberries evenly into indentations in Pavlovas, and top with whipped cream; garnish with mint leaves.

Cranberry-Almond Streusel Cake

SERVES **12 TO 16** HANDS-ON **45 MINUTES**
TOTAL **2 HOURS, 20 MINUTES, INCLUDING STREUSEL**

Don't limit this cake to the brunch table, it is lovely on a party table and is always a crowd-pleaser.

2 teaspoons baking powder	2 teaspoons orange zest (from 1 orange)
½ teaspoon baking soda	1 ½ teaspoons vanilla extract
½ teaspoon kosher salt	½ teaspoon almond extract
2 ½ cups (9 ⅜ ounces) bleached cake flour	12 ounces (3 cups) fresh or frozen cranberries
¾ cup (6 ounces) unsalted butter, softened	Almond Streusel (recipe follows)
1 cup granulated sugar	½ cup chopped whole natural almonds, toasted
¾ cup packed light brown sugar	½ cup jarred sea salt caramel sauce
3 large eggs	
1 ¼ cups sour cream	

1 Preheat oven to 350°F. Grease and flour a 10 ½-inch Bundt pan or 10-inch tube pan. Whisk together baking powder, baking soda, salt, and 2 ¼ cups plus 2 tablespoons of the flour in a medium bowl. Set aside.

2 Combine butter, granulated sugar, and brown sugar in the bowl of a heavy-duty stand mixer fitted with paddle attachment; beat on medium speed until light and fluffy, about 5 minutes. Add eggs, 1 at a time, beating well after each addition. Stir in sour cream, orange zest, and extracts. Gradually add flour mixture, beating on low speed just until blended after each addition.

3 Toss together cranberries and remaining 2 tablespoons cake flour in a small bowl until coated. Fold cranberries into batter. Pour half of batter into prepared pan; smooth batter, and top with Almond Streusel. Pour remaining batter over streusel, and smooth batter.

4 Bake in preheated oven until golden brown and a wooden pick inserted in center comes out clean, 50 minutes to 1 hour. Cool cake in pan on a wire rack 10 minutes. Remove cake from pan to wire rack, and let cool at least 30 minutes before serving. Combine almonds and 2 tablespoons of the caramel sauce; arrange on top of cake. Drizzle with remaining caramel sauce.

Almond Streusel

¼ cup packed light brown sugar	¼ teaspoon table salt
¼ cup bleached cake flour	1 cup chopped almonds
½ teaspoon ground cinnamon	2 tablespoons unsalted butter, melted

Stir together brown sugar, flour, cinnamon, and salt in a small bowl. Stir in almonds and butter until crumbly. Makes 1 ½ cups

VARIATION

Caramel Apple Streusel Cake

Omit orange zest, almond extract, and powdered sugar. Prepare recipe as directed, substituting **2 ½ cups peeled and chopped Granny Smith apples** (from 2 medium apples) for cranberries in cake and substituting **chopped pecans** for almonds in streusel. Drizzle cooled cake with **½ cup warm sea salt caramel sauce** (such as Stonewall Kitchen) just before serving. SERVES **12 TO 16**

Share

BIG FLUFFY
VANILLA
BEAN
MARSHMALLOWS

SUGAR & SPICE

HOMEMADE GIFTS FROM THE KITCHEN ARE A LONG-STANDING HOLIDAY TRADITION AND ARE AS MEANINGFUL TO MAKE WITH THOSE WE LOVE AS THEY ARE TO SHARE WITH NEIGHBORS, FRIENDS, COLLEAGUES, AND CLASSMATES.

SPICY SMOKED MARCONA ALMONDS

Spicy Cheddar-Pecan Rugelach

SERVES **48** HANDS-ON **30 MINUTES**
TOTAL **3 HOURS, 30 MINUTES, INCLUDING 2 HOURS
CHILLING**

Flaky pastry enveloping spicy cheese and pecans is all the goodness of cheese straws only richer. These can be made ahead and frozen. Just pop in the oven before guests arrive.

- 2 cups (about 8 ½ ounces) all-purpose flour
- 1 cup (8 ounces) cold unsalted butter, diced
- 12 ounces cold cream cheese, diced and divided
- ¾ teaspoon kosher salt
- 4 ounces sharp Cheddar cheese, finely shredded (about 1 ½ cups)
- 1 cup finely chopped toasted pecans
- ½ cup fresh flat-leaf parsley leaves and tender stems, finely chopped
- 1 teaspoon hot sauce (such as Cholula or Tabasco)
- 1 teaspoon paprika
- ½ teaspoon black pepper
- ¼ teaspoon cayenne pepper
- 1 large egg, beaten

1 Pulse flour, butter, 8 ounces of the cream cheese, and ½ teaspoon of the salt in a food processor until dough comes together and pulls away from sides of bowl, about 10 to 15 pulses.

2 Divide dough into 4 portions; shape each portion into a disk, and wrap each disk in plastic wrap. Refrigerate at least 2 hours or up to 24 hours.

3 Let remaining 4 ounces cream cheese stand at room temperature until softened. Preheat oven to 350°F. Stir together softened cream cheese, Cheddar, pecans, parsley, hot sauce, paprika, black pepper, cayenne, and remaining ¼ teaspoon salt in a large bowl until thoroughly blended.

4 Unwrap 1 portion of dough at a time, and roll disk into a 9-inch circle. Spread about ½ cup cheese mixture evenly over dough circle. Using a pizza wheel or sharp knife, cut circle into 12 triangles. Gently roll up each triangle, starting from the widest end and rolling toward the narrow end. Transfer rolled rugelachs to parchment paper-lined rimmed baking sheets. Brush rugelachs with beaten egg. Repeat procedure with remaining dough disks.

5 Bake in preheated oven until golden brown, 23 to 27 minutes. Let cool on baking sheets 5 minutes before transferring to wire racks to cool completely, about 30 minutes. Store in an airtight container at room temperature up to 7 days.

Big Fluffy Vanilla Bean Marshmallows

MAKES **2 DOZEN** HANDS-ON **30 MINUTES**
TOTAL **6 HOURS, 30 MINUTES, INCLUDING 6 HOURS
STANDING**

People are always impressed when you show up with homemade marshmallows. If only they knew how fun and easy they were to make! These are great for fireplace s'mores or floating in a steaming mug of hot cocoa.

- Powdered sugar
- ¾ cup cold water
- 3 (¼-ounce) envelopes unflavored gelatin
- 2 cups granulated sugar
- ⅔ cup light corn syrup
- ¼ teaspoon table salt
- 1 vanilla bean pod, halved lengthwise

1 Line a 13- x 9-inch pan with parchment paper, allowing 2 to 3 inches to extend over sides. Coat parchment paper in pan with cooking spray, and dust with powdered sugar.

2 Place ½ cup cold water in bowl of a heavy-duty stand mixer fitted with whisk attachment. Sprinkle gelatin over water, and let stand 5 minutes.

3 Combine granulated sugar, corn syrup, salt, and remaining ¼ cup water in a medium-size, heavy-bottomed saucepan. Cook over medium-high, stirring occasionally, until mixture begins to boil. Reduce heat to medium, and boil, without stirring, until a candy thermometer registers 240°F, about 10 minutes.

4 With mixer running on low speed, carefully and slowly pour boiling sugar mixture into gelatin mixture. Increase speed to high, and beat 6 minutes. Scrape vanilla beans into mixture, and beat until mixture stiffens, 6 to 7 more minutes. Pour mixture into prepared pan, smoothing with an offset spatula. Let stand, uncovered, at room temperature at least 6 hours or overnight.

5 Turn out marshmallow mixture onto a surface lightly dusted with powdered sugar. Peel off paper, and dust entire surface of marshmallow with additional powdered sugar. Use a lightly greased sharp knife to cut marshmallow into 2-inch squares. Coat all sides of marshmallows with powdered sugar. Store in an airtight container up to 2 weeks.

Ginger-Spice Pinecone Cookies

These thin, spicy gingersnaps are a festive treat when stacked to create pinecones, but they are also delicious crumbled to create gingersnap tart crusts or enjoyed with afternoon tea.

1 Combine butter and brown sugar in the bowl of a heavy-duty stand mixer fitted with paddle attachment. Beat on medium speed until lightened in color, 2 to 3 minutes. Add molasses and vanilla, and beat on medium speed until blended, about 2 minutes.

2 Whisk together flour, salt, baking soda, cinnamon, ginger, cloves, nutmeg, and allspice in a large bowl. With mixer running on low speed, gradually add flour mixture to molasses mixture, beating just until blended after each addition and stopping to scrape down sides as needed.

3 Divide dough in half, shape each into a disk, wrap tightly in plastic wrap, and refrigerate at least 3 hours or up to 3 days.

4 Preheat oven to 375°F. Roll out dough on a lightly floured surface (or between 2 layers of parchment paper) to ⅛-inch thickness. Using 5 graduated flower-shaped cookie cutters, varying in widths between 1 and 4 inches, cut out cookies. (You will have about 10 of each size cookie, rerolling dough once.) Place larger cookies on a parchment paper-lined baking sheet, and place smaller cookies on a separate parchment paper-lined baking sheet. Bake cookies in preheated oven until firm and beginning to darken around edges; small cookies 5 to 8 minutes, large cookies 8 to 10 minutes. Let cool on baking sheets 5 minutes before transferring to wire racks to cool completely, about 30 minutes.

5 In a small bowl, whisk together powdered sugar and water. Use an offset spatula or the back of a spoon to dab a little icing on the center of 1 large cooled cookie. Top with another cookie of the same size, rotating so petals do not overlap. Repeat procedure with cookies the next size down, continuing until smallest cookies are on top of stack. (There should be 10 cookies, 2 of each size, in each pinecone stack.) Dust pinecones with additional powdered sugar.

MAKES **ABOUT 5 "PINECONES,"
EACH USING 10 COOKIES**
HANDS-ON **45 MINUTES**
TOTAL **3 HOURS, 45 MINUTES,
INCLUDING 3 HOURS CHILLING**

---

6 tablespoons (3 ounces) unsalted butter, softened

¼ cup packed light brown sugar

⅔ cup unsulphured molasses

1 teaspoon vanilla extract

2 ½ cups (about 10 ⅝ ounces) all-purpose flour

1 teaspoon kosher salt

½ teaspoon baking soda

½ teaspoon ground cinnamon

½ teaspoon ground ginger

½ teaspoon ground cloves

¼ teaspoon freshly grated nutmeg

¼ teaspoon ground allspice

½ cup (2 ounces) powdered sugar, plus more for dusting

1 tablespoon water

Spicy Smoked Marcona Almonds

MAKES **2 CUPS** HANDS-ON **10 MINUTES**
TOTAL **45 MINUTES**

A nice addition to a cocktail hour cheese or charcuterie board, these sweet spiced nuts are a great gift for the party host.

2 cups raw Marcona almonds

1 tablespoon unsalted butter, melted

2 tablespoons pure maple syrup

3 tablespoons light brown sugar

1/2 teaspoon ground cinnamon

1/2 teaspoon cayenne pepper

1 teaspoon smoked paprika

1 teaspoon chili powder

1/2 teaspoon chipotle chile powder

1 teaspoon kosher salt

1 Preheat oven to 350°F. Line a rimmed baking sheet with aluminum foil, and coat foil with cooking spray. Spread almonds in a single layer on prepared baking sheet, and bake in preheated oven 10 minutes, tossing halfway through bake time.

2 Meanwhile, stir together butter, syrup, brown sugar, cinnamon, cayenne, paprika, chili powder, chipotle chile powder, and salt in a large bowl.

3 Transfer warm almonds to butter mixture, tossing to coat. Return coated almonds to baking sheet, spreading almonds in a single layer. Bake until browned, 14 to 16 minutes, stirring often. Let almonds cool completely on baking sheet on a wire rack before serving, about 20 minutes. Store in an airtight container at room temperature up to 7 days.

Ginger-Rosemary Syrup

MAKES ABOUT **3 CUPS** HANDS-ON **5 MINUTES**
TOTAL **30 MINUTES**

Cocktail buffs and seltzer addicts will love this warm and wintry syrup to embellish their drinks. It pairs well with bourbon but also won praise in a Moscow Mule and a margarita. Try it in a cup of hot orange pekoe tea too.

2 cups granulated sugar

2 cups water

2 (4-inch) rosemary sprigs

1 (1-inch) piece fresh ginger, peeled and sliced

1 Stir together all ingredients in a medium-size, heavy-bottomed saucepan. Bring mixture to a boil over medium-high. Reduce heat to low, and simmer 5 minutes.

2 Remove mixture from heat, cover, and let stand 20 minutes.

3 Pour mixture through a fine wire-mesh strainer into an airtight container. Store in refrigerator up to 2 months.

jezebel sauce

Jezebel Sauce

MAKES ABOUT **4 ½ CUPS** HANDS-ON **10 MINUTES**
TOTAL **10 MINUTES**

This mid-century sauce of community cookbook fame never goes out of style. It adds sweet heat to pork but is also tasty paired with sharp Cheddar cheese and crackers, slathered on a warm ham biscuit, or used as a glaze for wings. Spoon it over a log of goat cheese (or block of cream cheese) and serve with crackers for an appetizer that is ready in minutes.

2 cups pineapple
  preserves
2 cups apple jelly
½ cup prepared
  horseradish

⅓ cup Dijon mustard
1 tablespoon coarsely
  ground black pepper

Stir together all ingredients in a large bowl. Spoon mixture into 6- to 8-ounce jars with tight-fitting lids; cover jars with lids, and refrigerate until ready to use. Store in refrigerator up to 1 month.

Mincemeat

MAKES **ABOUT 4 CUPS** HANDS-ON **25 MINUTES**
TOTAL **2 HOURS, 15 MINUTES**

All the great flavors of fall—apple, cinnamon, clove—are woven into this traditional holiday favorite. Use this delicious mix in a double crust pie, folded into quick bread batters, or to fill thumbprint cookies.

2 apples, peeled and
  diced (about 8 ounces
  each)
1 tablespoon lemon zest,
  plus ¼ cup fresh juice
  (from 2 lemons)
2 tablespoons
  orange zest, plus
  7 tablespoons fresh
  juice (from 1 large
  orange)
½ cup currants
½ cup golden raisins
½ cup dried dates,
  chopped (about 8)
½ cup dried cherries
¼ cup chopped
  crystallized ginger

⅓ cup finely chopped
  pecans
⅓ cup (2 ⅔ ounces)
  unsalted butter, cubed
1 cup packed light brown
  sugar
⅓ cup pure maple syrup
½ teaspoon ground
  cinnamon
½ teaspoon ground
  cloves
½ teaspoon freshly
  grated nutmeg
½ teaspoon ground
  allspice
¼ teaspoon black
  pepper
¼ cup brandy

1 Combine apples, lemon zest and juice, orange zest and juice, currants, raisins, dates, cherries, ginger, pecans, butter, brown sugar, syrup, cinnamon, cloves, nutmeg, allspice, and pepper in a large saucepan. Cook over medium, stirring often, until mixture comes to a boil. Reduce heat to medium-low, and simmer, stirring occasionally, until mixture is thick and fruit is very tender, 45 to 50 minutes.

2 Remove from heat, and stir in brandy. Spoon mincemeat into 6- to 8-ounce jars with tight-fitting lids. Cover with lids, and let cool to room temperature, about 1 hour. Store in refrigerator up to 2 weeks.

Cranberry Jam

MAKES **ABOUT 4 ½ CUPS** HANDS-ON **15 MINUTES**
TOTAL **2 HOURS, 35 MINUTES**

This sweet-tart jam is balanced with the brightness of orange zest and the warmth of vanilla bean. The longer this cooks, the thicker it will get.

4 cups fresh cranberries
1 tablespoon orange zest, plus ½ cup fresh juice (from 1 orange)
4 cups granulated sugar
1 vanilla bean pod, split lengthwise

1 Combine cranberries, orange zest and juice, and sugar in a large heavy-bottomed saucepan. Scrape seeds from split vanilla bean into cranberry mixture, and stir until blended. Cook over medium-high, stirring often, until cranberries soften and begin to burst, 10 to 15 minutes.

2 Remove from heat, and process cranberry mixture with an immersion blender until smooth or to desired consistency.

3 Return saucepan to stove, and cook over medium, stirring occasionally, until slightly thickened and mixture coats the back of a spoon, 10 to 15 minutes.

4 Pour cranberry mixture into 6- to 8-ounce jars with tight-fitting lids. Cover with lids, and let cool to room temperature, about 2 hours. Store in refrigerator up to 3 weeks.

Cranberry Jam Thumbprint Cookies

MAKES **4 ½ DOZEN** HANDS-ON **30 MINUTES**
TOTAL **1 HOUR, 30 MINUTES**

These pretty cookies beg to be enjoyed with a cup of eggnog and are perfect on a plate for Santa.

1 cup (8 ounces) unsalted butter, softened
⅔ cup granulated sugar
2 large egg yolks
1 teaspoon vanilla extract
2 ¼ cups (about 9 ⅝ ounces) all-purpose flour
1 teaspoon kosher salt
½ teaspoon ground cinnamon
¼ teaspoon ground ginger
1 cup walnuts, very finely chopped
1 cup pecans, very finely chopped
5 tablespoons Cranberry Jam (at left) or store-bought jam

1 Preheat oven to 350°F. Beat butter and sugar with a heavy-duty stand mixer fitted with paddle attachment on medium speed until creamy, 2 to 3 minutes. Add egg yolks, 1 at a time, beating just until blended after each addition and stopping to scrape down sides as needed. Beat in vanilla on low speed until blended.

2 In a medium bowl, whisk together the flour, salt, cinnamon, and ginger. With the mixer on low speed, gradually add the flour mixture to the butter mixture, beating until blended after each addition and stopping to scrape down sides as needed. Stir in ¼ cup each of the walnuts and pecans.

3 Combine remaining walnuts and pecans in a shallow bowl. Roll dough into 1-inch balls. Roll balls in nut mixture to coat, and place on parchment paper-lined baking sheets, leaving about 2 inches of space between each. Using your thumb, gently make an indentation in the center of each cookie; fill indentations with Cranberry Jam (about ¼ teaspoon each). Bake in preheated oven until lightly browned, 12 to 14 minutes. Cool on baking sheets 5 minutes. Transfer to wire racks to cool completely, about 10 minutes. Store in an airtight container at room temperature up to 3 days.

Cranberry Jam

Rocky Road Cookies

MAKES 3 DOZEN HANDS-ON 20 MINUTES TOTAL 50 MINUTES

Be sure to use regular unsweetened cocoa because the extra dark cocoa may turn these cookies an unattractive purple-red. The only thing better than these is these with a tall glass of milk.

1 cup (8 ounces) unsalted butter, softened
1 cup packed dark brown sugar
½ cup granulated sugar
2 teaspoons vanilla extract
2 large eggs
2 cups (8 ½ ounces) all-purpose flour
1 teaspoon baking soda

2 teaspoons cornstarch
½ teaspoon kosher salt
1 cup unsweetened cocoa
2 tablespoons whole milk
1 ½ cups semisweet chocolate chips
2 cups toasted pecans, finely chopped
1 ½ cups miniature marshmallows

1 Preheat oven to 350°F. Beat butter and sugars with a heavy-duty stand mixer fitted with paddle attachment on medium speed until fluffy, 3 to 4 minutes. Add vanilla, and beat on low speed until blended. Add eggs, 1 at a time, beating just until blended after each addition and stopping to scrape down sides of bowl as needed.

2 In a medium bowl, whisk together flour, baking soda, cornstarch, salt, and cocoa. With mixer running on low speed, gradually add flour mixture to butter mixture, beating just until blended after each addition. Add milk, beating just until combined (dough will be sticky). Fold in chocolate chips.

3 Place pecans in a shallow bowl. Using a 1- to 1 ½-inch cookie scoop, shape dough into balls, and roll in pecans. Place balls on a parchment paper-lined baking sheet, leaving 1 inch of space between each. Bake in preheated oven for 8 minutes. Remove baking sheet from oven, and press 3 marshmallows into the top of each cookie. Return to oven, and bake 5 more minutes. Cool on baking sheet 5 minutes; transfer to a wire rack to cool completely. Serve cookies slightly warm or at room temperature. Store cooled cookies in an airtight container at room temperature up to 2 days.

Need it? Find it!

We wish to thank the following vendors and artisans whose products were photographed in this book. Source information is accurate at the time of publication. Many items featured in this book are one-of-a-kind or privately owned so not sourced.

Accent Decor

Accents de Ville

Allstate Floral

Ameritiques Ltd.

Appelman & Schauben

Apropos, Inc.

Arte Italica

Atlanta Silver & Antiques

Be Home, Inc.

BIDK Home

Blue Pheasant

Bobo Intriguing Objects

Bromberg's

Casa Bugatti USA

Christian Mosso & Associates, Inc.

Creative Co-op / Bloomingville

CVS Pharmacy

Designs Combined Inc. (DCI)

d.stevens

Etsy.com

Etú Home

Europe 2 You

Farmhouse Pottery

Gardens of the Blue Ridge Inc.

Global Views

Hedgerow Antiques

Hobby Lobby

HomArt

HomeGoods

K&K Interiors

Leaf & Petal

Linen Way Inc.

Melrose International

Michaels Stores

Montes Doggett

Paper Source

Park Hill Collection

Shea's Wildflower Company

Spence Collection Antiques

Table Matters

Tozai Home

Target

T.J. Maxx

Two's Company Inc.

Very Vintage Villa

Walmart

West Elm

Zodax

Thanks to these contributors

We appreciate the contributions of these local businesses

At Home

Bromberg's

Chelsea Antique Mall

Davis Wholesale Florist

Hall's Birmingham Wholesale Florist

Leaf & Petal

Oak Street Garden Shop

Table Matters

Tricia's Treasures

Thanks to the following homeowners

The Jones Family

The Miles Family

The Russell Family

The Stanford Family

Mt. Laurel

General Index

Metric Equivalents

The recipes that appear in this cookbook use the standard United States method for measuring liquid and dry or solid ingredients (teaspoons, tablespoons, and cups). The information on this page is provided to help cooks outside the U.S. successfully use these recipes. All equivalents are approximate.

Metric Equivalents for Different Types of Ingredients

A standard cup measure of a dry or solid ingredient will vary in weight depending on the type of ingredient. A standard cup of liquid is the same volume for any type of liquid. Use the following chart when converting standard cup measures to grams (weight) or milliliters (volume).

Standard Cup	Fine Powder (ex. flour)	Grain (ex. rice)	Granular (ex. sugar)	Liquid Solids (ex. butter)	Liquid (ex. milk)
1	140 g	150 g	190 g	200 g	240 ml
3/4	105 g	113 g	143 g	150 g	180 ml
2/3	93 g	100 g	125 g	133 g	160 ml
1/2	70 g	75 g	95 g	100 g	120 ml
1/3	47 g	50 g	63 g	67 g	80 ml
1/4	35 g	38 g	48 g	50 g	60 ml
1/8	18 g	19 g	24 g	25 g	30 ml

Useful Equivalents for Liquid Ingredients by Volume

1/4 tsp					=	1 ml	
1/2 tsp					=	2 ml	
1 tsp					=	5 ml	
3 tsp	=	1 Tbsp		= 1/2 fl oz	=	15 ml	
		2 Tbsp	= 1/8 cup	= 1 fl oz	=	30 ml	
		4 Tbsp	= 1/4 cup	= 2 fl oz	=	60 ml	
		5 1/3 Tbsp	= 1/3 cup	= 3 fl oz	=	80 ml	
		8 Tbsp	= 1/2 cup	= 4 fl oz	=	120 ml	
		10 2/3 Tbsp	= 2/3 cup	= 5 fl oz	=	160 ml	
		12 Tbsp	= 3/4 cup	= 6 fl oz	=	180 ml	
		16 Tbsp	= 1 cup	= 8 fl oz	=	240 ml	
		1 pt	= 2 cups	= 16 fl oz	=	480 ml	
		1 qt	= 4 cups	= 32 fl oz	=	960 ml	
				33 fl oz	=	1000 ml	= 1 l

Useful Equivalents for Dry Ingredients by Weight

(To convert ounces to grams, multiply the number of ounces by 30.)

1 oz	=	1/16 lb	=	30 g
4 oz	=	1/4 lb	=	120 g
8 oz	=	1/2 lb	=	240 g
12 oz	=	3/4 lb	=	360 g
16 oz	=	1 lb	=	480 g

Useful Equivalents for Length

(To convert inches to centimeters, multiply the number of inches by 2.5.)

1 in				= 2.5 cm	
6 in	= 1/2 ft			= 15 cm	
12 in	= 1 ft			= 30 cm	
36 in	= 3 ft	= 1 yd	= 90 cm	
40 in			= 100 cm	= 1 m

Useful Equivalents for Cooking/Oven Temperatures

	Fahrenheit	Celsius	Gas Mark
Freeze water	32° F	0° C	
Room temperature	68° F	20° C	
Boil water	212° F	100° C	
Bake	325° F	160° C	
	350° F	180° C	3
	375° F	190° C	4
	400° F	200° C	5
	425° F	220° C	6
Broil	450° F	230° C	7
			8
			Grill

Recipe Index

Executive Editor: Katherine Cobbs
Project Editors: Diane Keener, Lacie Pinyan
Photo Director: Paden Reich
Designer: Matt Ryan
Photographers: Antonis Achilleos, Becky Luigart-Stayner
Prop Stylist: Kay E. Clarke
Food Stylists: Margaret Monroe Dickey,
Kellie Gerber Kelley, Tina Bell Stamos
Recipe Developers and Testers: Allene Arnold,
Robin Bashinsky, Mary Claire Britton, Adam Dolge,
Adam Hickman, Julia G. Levy, Pam Lolley, Robby Melvin,
Liz Mervosh, Ivy Odom, Karen Schroeder-Rankin,
Anna Theoktisto, Deb Wise
Contributing Production Manager: Greg A. Amason
Contributing Copy Editors: Donna Baldone,
Rebecca Brennan, Julie Doll
Contributing Indexer: Mary Ann Laurens

ISBN-13: 978-0-8487-5973-5
ISSN: 0747-7791

First Edition 2019
Printed in the United States of America
10 9 8 7 6 5 4 3 2 1

Interested in more books from the brands you love?
Whether you enjoy cooking, gardening, or decorating,
you'll find a wealth of how-to books that can be shipped
straight to your door. Call 1-800-826-4707 for more
information.

Holiday Planner

This handy planner will help you stay on track
all season long. From decorating and table-setting
tips to gift and card lists, everything you need
to plan the perfect holiday is at your fingertips.

November 2019

SUNDAY	MONDAY	TUESDAY	WEDNESDAY
3	4	5	6
10	11	12	13
17	18	19	20
24	25	26	27

THURSDAY	FRIDAY	SATURDAY
	1	2
7	8	9
14	15	16
21	22	23
Thanksgiving 28	29	30

Holiday-Ready Pantry

Be prepared for seasonal cooking and baking by stocking up on these items.

- ☐ Assorted coffees, teas, hot chocolate, and eggnog
- ☐ Wine, beer, and soft drinks
- ☐ Granulated, brown, and powdered sugars
- ☐ Ground allspice, cinnamon, cloves, ginger, and nutmeg
- ☐ Baking soda and baking powder
- ☐ Seasonal fresh herbs
- ☐ Baking chocolate
- ☐ Semisweet chocolate chips
- ☐ Assorted nuts
- ☐ Flaked coconut
- ☐ Sweetened condensed milk and evaporated milk
- ☐ Whipping cream
- ☐ Jams, jellies, and preserves
- ☐ Raisins, cranberries, and other fresh or dried fruits
- ☐ Canned pumpkin
- ☐ Frozen/refrigerated bread dough, biscuits, and croissants

Holiday Hotlines

Use these toll-free telephone numbers when you need answers to last-minute food questions.

USDA Meat & Poultry Hotline: 1-888-674-6854

FDA Center for Food Safety: 1-888-723-3366

Butterball Turkey Talk-Line: 1-800-288-8372

Betty Crocker (General Mills): 1-800-446-1898

December 2019

SUNDAY	MONDAY	TUESDAY	WEDNESDAY
1	2	3	4
8	9	10	11
15	16	17	18
22	23	Christmas Eve 24	Christmas 25
29	30	New Year's Eve 31	

THURSDAY	FRIDAY	SATURDAY
5	6	7
12	13	14
19	20	21
Boxing Day 26	27	28

Helpful Hostess Tips

Use these shortcuts and tips to make your holiday get-togethers go off without a hitch.

ALWAYS EXPECT THE UNEXPECTED. Should red wine spill, be prepared with your favorite stain remover. We love Wine Away, available through www.amazon.com.

IN CASE IT RAINS, keep a few extra umbrellas on hand so your friends don't get soaked running to their cars.

THINK ABOUT PARKING AHEAD OF TIME. Too many extra cars on the street can be dangerous. Check with your neighbors to see if their driveways may be available.

IF SOMEONE ASKS TO HELP, don't be afraid to take them up on the generous offer.

ASK FRIENDS TO ARRIVE with a favorite playlist so you have an eclectic mix to choose from.

A LITTLE PREP WORK GOES A LONG WAY. Before guests arrive, uncork all the wine bottles, light candles, and put coffee and water in your machine.

DOUBLE CHECK THAT YOU HAVE PLENTY of extra hangers in your coat closet. Or use a spare bedroom to store coats, hats, and purses.

WHEN HOSTING A LARGE CROWD, consider renting china, silverware, glasses, and more from a local party or event store. You'll be amazed at how low the prices are if you stick to the basics.

Decorating Planner

Here's a list of details and finishing touches you can use to
tailor a picture-perfect house this holiday season.

Decorative materials needed

FROM THE YARD ....

FROM AROUND THE HOUSE ....

FROM THE STORE ....

OTHER ....

Holiday decorations

FOR THE TABLE ....

FOR THE DOOR..

FOR THE MANTEL..

FOR THE STAIRCASE ....

OTHER ....

YOUR BEST CHRISTMAS TREE EVER

Several tricks can make your tree sparkle better than ever. Invite these ideas into your
tree-trimming traditions, and then sit back and enjoy your gorgeous work of art.

Skip the Usual Metal Stand
This year, use a natural woven basket to hold your
Christmas tree. You'll likely still need to support the
trunk inside the basket with a stand, but the results
are much more beautiful.

More Bang with Bulbs
Lighting the tree doesn't have to be the dreaded task
of the season. Go ahead and spring for new lights—
there's a much better chance they'll work. Mix large
bulbs with smaller ones for extra twinkle, and be
sure to use a surge protector with multiple outlets
so you don't overload your receptacles with a gaggle
of extension cords. Place the lights on your tree at
night so it's easier to see where you need to add or
take away a strand.

The Real Fun Begins
Start with your largest ornaments first and arrange
them all around the tree. If they're extra heavy,
secure them to the tree with florist wire. Sometimes
oversize baubles tend to slip off branches.

Tie inexpensive Christmas balls and metallic
jingle bells together with florist wire to create an
interesting cluster of color.

Update Your Look
Give your tree a fresh look year after year by editing
your ornaments. Maybe you want a color theme,
such as all red and gold; then display the rest around
the house.

Experiment with Tree Toppers
Bunch fresh holly from the yard and large gold
temple bells on top of the tree for a bold use of
traditional materials. Fresh flowers are another nice
decorating alternative to the traditional star. Or try
an oversize bow in red velvet.

Final Touches for a Fantastic Tree
When you're just about done, add some festive
ribbon! Use as many colors as you like. Weave ribbon
streamers down and around your tree, and secure
with florist wire in a few spots.

Deck the Halls

Bring joy and merriment into your home with these fun and easy decorating ideas.

Add Color to Your Front Door

Accent a bright white door with the deep colors of an evergreen wreath and garland. Tie on extra-wide red ribbons to complete the Christmas look and add graphic punch. Twinkling lights add a soft glow at night and allow the door and decor to be seen from the street.

Picture-Perfect Garland

Deck your halls with a distinctive—and decidedly charming—family photo garland. Just cut circular shapes from copies of your favorite photos, and glue them to the backs of large wooden curtain rings. Use ribbon to attach the rings to a garland for your stairs or mantel. You could even hang them on your tree. No doubt, Santa will feel most welcome when he sees all those smiling faces.

Fill Cylinders with Ornaments

Use spray paint to add a shimmery touch to pinecones, acorns, or round glass ornaments. Displayed en masse in tall glass vases, they become instant and easy Christmas accents.

Put Out Pretty Pillows

Make a quick switch from everyday to holiday by swapping out your throw pillows. It's an easy and affordable way to redecorate a room and change your look for the Christmas season.

String Lights and Greenery

Disguise unsightly wires from string lights by winding them around a column or post with Christmas greenery or garland.

Create an Arrangement with Fruit and Greenery

Use a glass hurricane or vase to create an arrangement that will last throughout the Christmas season by filling the jar with a layer of limes, red holly berries, and orange citrus. Top it off with stems of greenery.

White and Bright

Here's a Christmas surprise: lilies for your dining room table. Though usually associated with spring, these crisp, snowy flowers with their star-shaped blooms couldn't be more perfect for yuletide celebrations. Available year-round, they add elegance and fragrance to any setting. To create an arrangement, buy one long stem from a local florist. Look for a stem that has one bloom open and several others beginning to unfurl. Clip the flowers from the stem, and place them in a vase. Add water daily, and the flowers should last for a week.

Festive Floor Pillows

Create a comfy spot for kids to open presents on Christmas morning! Whip out your sewing machine and make a set of festive floor cushions, monogrammed with children's names.

Party Planner

Stay on top of your party plans with this time-saving menu organizer.

GUESTS	WHAT THEY'RE BRINGING	SERVING PIECES NEEDED
	☐ appetizer ☐ beverage ☐ bread ☐ main dish ☐ side dish ☐ dessert	
	☐ appetizer ☐ beverage ☐ bread ☐ main dish ☐ side dish ☐ dessert	
	☐ appetizer ☐ beverage ☐ bread ☐ main dish ☐ side dish ☐ dessert	
	☐ appetizer ☐ beverage ☐ bread ☐ main dish ☐ side dish ☐ dessert	
	☐ appetizer ☐ beverage ☐ bread ☐ main dish ☐ side dish ☐ dessert	
	☐ appetizer ☐ beverage ☐ bread ☐ main dish ☐ side dish ☐ dessert	
	☐ appetizer ☐ beverage ☐ bread ☐ main dish ☐ side dish ☐ dessert	
	☐ appetizer ☐ beverage ☐ bread ☐ main dish ☐ side dish ☐ dessert	
	☐ appetizer ☐ beverage ☐ bread ☐ main dish ☐ side dish ☐ dessert	
	☐ appetizer ☐ beverage ☐ bread ☐ main dish ☐ side dish ☐ dessert	
	☐ appetizer ☐ beverage ☐ bread ☐ main dish ☐ side dish ☐ dessert	
	☐ appetizer ☐ beverage ☐ bread ☐ main dish ☐ side dish ☐ dessert	
	☐ appetizer ☐ beverage ☐ bread ☐ main dish ☐ side dish ☐ dessert	
	☐ appetizer ☐ beverage ☐ bread ☐ main dish ☐ side dish ☐ dessert	
	☐ appetizer ☐ beverage ☐ bread ☐ main dish ☐ side dish ☐ dessert	
	☐ appetizer ☐ beverage ☐ bread ☐ main dish ☐ side dish ☐ dessert	

Party Guest List

....
....
....
....
....
....
....
....
....
....
....
....
....
....
....
....

Party To-Do List

....
....
....
....
....
....
....
....
....
....
....
....
....
....

Christmas Dinner Planner

Use this space to create a menu, to-do list, and guest list for your special holiday celebration.

Menu Ideas

....
....
....
....
....
....
....

Dinner To-Do List

....
....
....
....
....
....
....

Christmas Dinner Guest List

....
....
....
....
....
....
....
....
....

Pantry List

Grocery List

Gifts & Greetings

Keep up with family and friends' sizes, jot down gift ideas, and record purchases in this convenient chart. Also, use it to keep track of addresses for your Christmas card list.

Gift List and Size Charts

	GIFT PURCHASED/MADE	SENT

name ....

jeans_____ shirt_____ sweater_____ jacket_____ shoes_____ belt_____
blouse_____ skirt_____ slacks_____ dress_____ suit_____ coat_____
pajamas_____ robe_____ hat_____ gloves_____ ring_____

name ....

jeans_____ shirt_____ sweater_____ jacket_____ shoes_____ belt_____
blouse_____ skirt_____ slacks_____ dress_____ suit_____ coat_____
pajamas_____ robe_____ hat_____ gloves_____ ring_____

name ....

jeans_____ shirt_____ sweater_____ jacket_____ shoes_____ belt_____
blouse_____ skirt_____ slacks_____ dress_____ suit_____ coat_____
pajamas_____ robe_____ hat_____ gloves_____ ring_____

name ....

jeans_____ shirt_____ sweater_____ jacket_____ shoes_____ belt_____
blouse_____ skirt_____ slacks_____ dress_____ suit_____ coat_____
pajamas_____ robe_____ hat_____ gloves_____ ring_____

name ....

jeans_____ shirt_____ sweater_____ jacket_____ shoes_____ belt_____
blouse_____ skirt_____ slacks_____ dress_____ suit_____ coat_____
pajamas_____ robe_____ hat_____ gloves_____ ring_____

name ....

jeans_____ shirt_____ sweater_____ jacket_____ shoes_____ belt_____
blouse_____ skirt_____ slacks_____ dress_____ suit_____ coat_____
pajamas_____ robe_____ hat_____ gloves_____ ring_____

name ....

jeans_____ shirt_____ sweater_____ jacket_____ shoes_____ belt_____
blouse_____ skirt_____ slacks_____ dress_____ suit_____ coat_____
pajamas_____ robe_____ hat_____ gloves_____ ring_____

Christmas Card List

NAME	ADDRESS	SENT

Holiday Memories

Hold on to priceless Christmas memories forever with handwritten recollections of this season's magical moments.

Treasured Traditions

Keep track of your family's favorite holiday customs and pastimes on these lines.

....
....
....
....
....
....
....
....
....
....
....
....
....

Special Holiday Activities

What holiday events do you look forward to year after year? Write them down here.

....
....
....
....
....
....
....
....
....
....

Holiday Visits and Visitors

Keep a list of this year's holiday visitors.
Jot down friend and family news as well.

....
....
....
....
....
....
....
....
....
....
....
....
....
....
....
....
....
....
....
....
....
....
....

This Year's Favorite Recipes

Appetizers and Beverages...................................
....
....
....
....

Entrées...
....
....
....

Sides and Salads...
....
....
....

Cookies and Candies.......................................
....
....
....

Desserts...
....
....
....

Looking Ahead

Holiday Wrap-up

Use this checklist to record thank-you notes sent for holiday gifts and hospitality.

NAME	GIFT AND/OR EVENT	NOTE SENT
....	....	☐
....	....	☐
....	....	☐
....	....	☐
....	....	☐
....	....	☐
....	....	☐
....	....	☐
....	....	☐
....	....	☐
....	....	☐
....	....	☐
....	....	☐

Notes for Next Year

Write down your ideas for Christmas 2020 on the lines below.

....

....

....

....

....

....

....

....

....

....